THE
LANDS OF THE
BIBLE
TODAY

Experience 44 places in Scripture and photos

By DAVE BRANON

Our Daily Bread
Publishing™

The Lands of the Bible Today: Experience 44 Places in Scripture and Photos
© 2020 by Dave Branon

All rights reserved.

Requests for permission to quote from this book should be directed to: Permissions Department, Our Daily Bread Publishing, PO Box 3566, Grand Rapids, MI 49501, or contact us by email at permissionsdept@odb.org.

Scripture quotations, unless otherwise indicated, are taken from the Holy Bible, New International Version®, NIV®. Copyright © 1973, 1978, 1984, 2011 by Biblica, Inc.™ Used by permission of Zondervan. All rights reserved worldwide. www.zondervan.com.

Scripture quotations marked NASB are from the New American Standard Bible®, copyright © 1960, 1962, 1963, 1968, 1971, 1972, 1973, 1975, 1977, 1995 by The Lockman Foundation. Used by permission. (Lockman.org)

Scripture quotations marked NCV are from the New Century Version®. Copyright © 2005 by Thomas Nelson. Used by permission. All rights reserved.

Scripture quotations marked TLB are taken from The Living Bible copyright © 1971. Used by permission of Tyndale House Publishers, Inc., Carol Stream, Illinois 60188. All rights reserved.

Interior design by Steve Gier

Library of Congress Cataloging-in-Publication Data

Names: Branon, Dave, author.

Title: The lands of the Bible today : experience 44 places in scripture and photos / by Dave Branon. Description: Grand Rapids, Michigan : Our Daily Bread Publishing, [2020] | Includes bibliographical references. | Summary: "This visual tour of the Holy Land brings 44 places in that region up close and personal with beautiful photographs and interesting information"-- Provided by publisher.

Identifiers: LCCN 2020036575 | ISBN 9781640700512 (paperback)

Subjects: LCSH: Middle East--Description and travel. | Middle East--Pictorial works.

Classification: LCC DS108.5 .B67 2020 | DDC 220.9/1--dc23

LC record available at https://lccn.loc.gov/2020036575

Printed in the United States of America
21 22 23 24 25 26 27 / 8 7 6 5 4 3 2

Terry Bidgood / ODBM

Alex Soh / ODBM

Terry Bidgood / ODBM

CONTENTS

Terry Bidgood / ODBM

Introduction
FEELS LIKE I'VE BEEN THERE

Israel. The Promised Land. The Holy Land.

Whatever Christians call this treasured piece of real estate, it has a soft spot in the hearts of all who have a reverence and veneration for the Bible-related people, events, and life-changing stories that took place in this land. We can add to our interest level for all things biblical by considering also the places west of Israel and north of the Mediterranean that were evangelized in the first century after Jesus arose victoriously.

Like no other area of the world, Israel and the region around it have a natural familiarity to those of us who study the Bible and its stories. Some of us may know South America because of a trip there or because we have missionary friends

Terry Bidgood / ODBM

who serve there. Others of us know something of Europe or the Caribbean because we've vacationed there or know someone else who has.

But no other land has captured our thoughts and has imprinted itself on our minds like the land where Jesus and His disciples walked and where the first missionaries served.

Because many of us have been reading about these places for much of our lives, in a sense it seems as if we've been there.

But whether we have or haven't, it's always enjoyable to travel there in our imaginations—

to refamiliarize ourselves with towns and cities and areas that we can almost picture because we are so accustomed to hearing about them.

This book is intended to take us along to some of the key places we've heard about, read about, and studied and make them even more real to us. And whether we can or cannot take a tour of this valuable slice of our world, what we find in this book can help us place the locations in our mind's eye.

The section on each location provides a glimpse at its biblical background, some information about its actual location, and a look at what can be seen if one were to visit it today. Included in some of the vignettes is historical or archaeological information where appropriate.

Terry Bidgood / ODBM

The pictures that accompany some of the locales were taken by staff photographers of Our Daily Bread Ministries (ODBM), Terry Bidgood and Alex Soh.

Because I've been able to visit many of these locations, I have also included some short personal reflections of my favorite sites in Israel.[1] I hope that adds to your enjoyment of the book and your understanding of these significant places.

There is something magnificent about being in the land of Old Testament characters, of our Savior, and of His disciples—to realize they walked the same areas, sailed in the same seas, and in many cases trudged the same streets of places such as Capernaum, Ephesus, and Jerusalem. Becoming more familiar with these places doesn't make them any more real, but this additional knowledge can make them feel a bit more personal. I trust that the facts and reflections in this book will make the Bible story all the more realistic and exciting for you.

BEERSHEBA

1

*[Isaac] went up to **Beersheba**. That night the L<small>ORD</small> appeared to him and said, "I am the God of your father Abraham. Do not be afraid, for I am with you. . . ." Isaac built an altar there.* **GENESIS 26:23–25**

TEL BE'ER SHEVA: This UNESCO World Heritage site may contain, among other findings, the site of Abraham's well.
(Lev Levin / Shutterstock.com)

WHERE TO FIND IT IN THE BIBLE

Genesis 21:14, 31–33; 22:19; 26:33; 28:10; 46:1, 5; Judges 20:1; 1 Samuel 3:20; 8:2; 2 Samuel 24:7; 1 Kings 19:3; 2 Kings 12:1; 23:8; Amos 5:5; 8:14

KEY PASSAGES ABOUT BEERSHEBA

66 That place was called Beersheba, because the two men swore an oath there. **(GENESIS 21:31)**

66 When Samuel grew old, he appointed his sons as Israel's leaders. The name of his firstborn

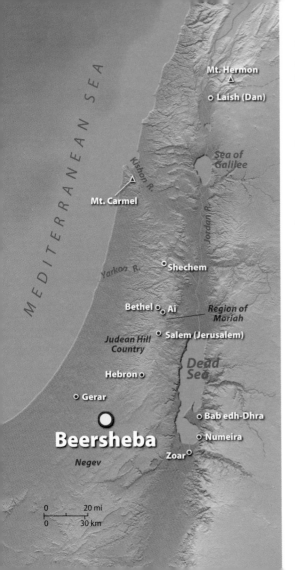

Mt. Hermon

Laish (Dan)

Sea of Galilee

Kishon R.

Mt. Carmel

Yarkos R.

Shechem

Jordan R.

Bethel Ai

Region of Moriah

Judean Hill Country

Salem (Jerusalem)

Hebron

Dead Sea

Gerar

Bab edh-Dhra

Numeira

Beersheba

Zoar

Negev

0 — 20 mi
0 — 30 km

MEDITERRANEAN SEA

was Joel and the name of his second was Abijah, and they served at Beersheba. **(1 SAMUEL 8:1–2)**

BIBLE STUFF THAT HAPPENED IN BEERSHEBA

● As with Dan in the north, several Scripture passages use Beersheba as a geographic marker that indicates the southernmost part of the Promised Land.

● Abraham made a treaty at Beersheba with Abimelek and Phicol, and he planted a tamarisk tree there.

● Isaac visited Beersheba, and God spoke to him there, reminding him that He was the God of his father Abraham. Isaac built an altar at Beersheba, pitched a tent there, and dug a well.

● Jacob also spent time at Beersheba. He offered sacrifices there to the God of his father Isaac.

● Samuel's sons Joel and Abijah served as judges in Beersheba.

● After his success at Mount Carmel, Elijah received a threat from Queen Jezebel. "Elijah was afraid and ran for his life" **(1 KINGS 19:3)** and ended up in Beersheba—about 150 miles away.

● During the spiritual restoration under the leadership of Josiah, the high places of Beersheba were desecrated.

- After the end of the Babylonian captivity, some returning Hebrews settled in Beersheba.

WHERE TO FIND IT IN ISRAEL

Beersheba is 75 miles southwest of Jerusalem. An automobile trip from Jerusalem would take about an hour and a half. According to *Fodor's Essential Israel,* the route from Jerusalem starts at "Route 1 west to the Route 6 turnoff. Follow Route 6 southbound; after Kiryat Gat it turns into Route 40 south, which leads into Beersheba."[2]

THINGS TO SEE

◆ *Tel Be'er Sheva:* This UNESCO World Heritage site may contain the site of Abraham's well. Among the findings at Tel Beersheba is a tenth-century BC city gate and a Roman fortress.[3] Visitors can tour the excavated ruins at Tel Be'er Sheva in about two hours. Among the things to see are a town from about the time of King Hezekiah, a water cistern carved from rock, and houses and a palace from the eighth century BC. The tel is about four miles northeast of the modern city.

◆ *Horned altar:* At Tel Be'er Sheva the materials from the first horned altar to be found by archaeologists can be seen. The stones had been used later to build a wall, but scholars believe those stones once constituted an altar like the ones described in Exodus 29:12 and Leviticus 4:7.

◆ *Abraham's Well International Visitor Center* is located on the Beersheba River: Visitors are told the story of Abraham and the well that is central to his visit to Beersheba.

BEERSHEBA TODAY

Beersheba (also called Be'er Sheva) is a modern city with a population of about 200,000 people. It is home to Ben-Gurion University of the Negev, and it boasts an important high-tech industry.

*Now a man named Lazarus was sick. He was from **Bethany**, the village of Mary and her sister Martha.*

JOHN 11:1

2

BETHA

WHERE TO FIND IT IN THE BIBLE

Matthew 21:17; 26:6; Mark 11:1, 11–12; 14:3; Luke 19:29; 24:50; John 11:1, 18; 12:1

KEY PASSAGES ABOUT BETHANY

❝ Six days before the Passover, Jesus came to Bethany, where Lazarus lived, whom Jesus had raised from the dead. . . . Mary took about a pint of pure nard, an expensive perfume; she poured it on Jesus' feet and wiped his feet with her hair. **(JOHN 12:1,3)**

❝ Jesus entered Jerusalem and went into the temple courts. He looked around at everything, but since it was already late, he went out to Bethany with the Twelve. **(MARK 11:11)**

TOMB STEPS: Traditionally considered the tomb of Lazarus, perhaps this was Lazarus's first view upon hearing Jesus's voice. (Terry Bidgood / ODBM)

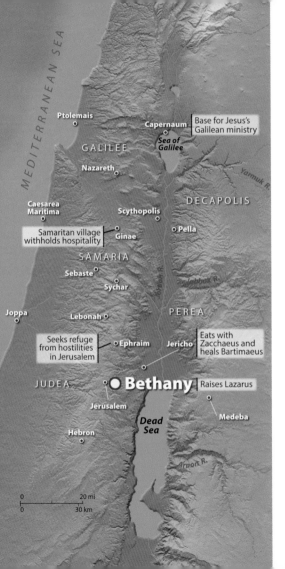

- **Ptolemais**
- **Capernaum** | Base for Jesus's Galilean ministry
- *Sea of Galilee*
- **GALILEE**
- **Nazareth**
- *Yarmuk R.*
- **DECAPOLIS**
- **Caesarea Maritima**
- **Scythopolis**
- *Jabbok R.*
- Samaritan village withholds hospitality | **Ginae** ○
- ○ **Pella**
- **SAMARIA**
- **Sebaste** ○
- **Sychar** ○
- **Joppa** ○
- **Lebonah** ○
- **PEREA**
- Seeks refuge from hostilities in Jerusalem | ○ **Ephraim**
- **Jericho** ○ | Eats with Zacchaeus and heals Bartimaeus
- **JUDEA** | ○ **Bethany** | Raises Lazarus
- **Jerusalem** ○
- *Dead Sea*
- **Hebron** ○
- **Medeba** ○
- *Arnon R.*
- 0 — 20 mi
- 0 — 30 km
- *MEDITERRANEAN SEA*

BIBLE STUFF THAT HAPPENED IN BETHANY

● Before Jesus's triumphal entry into Jerusalem, Jesus went through Bethany on His way.

● After Jesus's triumphant entry into Jerusalem and after driving out the money changers from the temple, Jesus went to Bethany to spend the night.

● At Bethany, Jesus visited the home of Simon the Leper. It was here that a woman anointed Jesus with expensive perfume from her alabaster jar.

Above: Bethany is now a town of a few thousand people. The traditional location of Lazarus's tomb is accessed by a series of steep, narrow stairs (Marion Doss / Creative Commons). *Left:* The Greek Orthodox church in Bethany (SeetheHolyLand.net / Creative Commons).

Politically, Bethany is part of the West Bank, under the Palestinian Authority, and it is blocked from access by a wall. Although it is near the Mount of Olives, a trip to Bethany requires a lengthy detour. A bus ride takes about forty minutes. Today the town is called Al-Azariyeh.

THINGS TO SEE

◆ *Tomb of Lazarus:* Just below a fourteenth-century mosque stands a sign with notices in various languages. The English on the sign says, "St. Lazarus Tomb." And it also requests, "Kindly show respect for the sanctity of this site." This site is the traditional location of the tomb from which Jesus called Lazarus forth. Nearby is a Franciscan church that was built in 1954. Pilgrims wishing to see the traditional site must go down a series of steep, narrow stairs to reach it.

◆ *Greek Orthodox church dedicated to Simon the Leper:* Nearby are ruins that some say are the remains of Simon's home.

● It appears that Jesus's ascension occurred in the "vicinity of Bethany" (**LUKE 24:50**).
● Most famously, Bethany was the town where Jesus raised his good friend Lazarus from the dead.

WHERE TO FIND IT IN ISRAEL

Although Bethany is just two miles outside Jerusalem, it is not as accessible from the city of David as it once was.

BETHLEHEM

3

*When the angels had left them and gone into heaven, the shepherds said to one another, "Let's go to **Bethlehem** and see this thing that has happened, which the Lord has told us about."*

LUKE 2:15

BETHLEHEM today is a Palestinian town with a large Arab Christian community. Non-Israeli tourists may have to show their passports at a checkpoint to get into the city, but they are usually welcomed to visit. The focal point of this former "little town of Bethlehem" is Manger Square, where the Church of the Nativity is located. It is accessible to tourists, but a passport is required. (Yacoub Hazboun / FreeImages.com)

WHERE TO FIND IT IN THE BIBLE

Genesis 35:19; Joshua 19:15; Judges 12:10; 17:7–9; 19; Ruth 1, 2, 4; 1 Samuel 17, 20; 2 Samuel 23; Ezra 2:21; Nehemiah 7:26; Micah 5:2; Matthew 2; Luke 2; John 7

KEY PASSAGES ABOUT BETHLEHEM

❝ But you, Bethlehem Ephrathah, though you are small among the clans of Judah, out of you will come for me one who will be ruler over Israel, whose origins are from of old, from ancient times. **(MICAH 5:2)**

❝ So Joseph went up from the town of Nazareth in Galilee to Judea, to Bethlehem the town of David, because he belonged to the house and line of David. He went there to register with Mary. . . . While they were there, the time came for the baby to be born, and she gave birth to her firstborn, a son. **(LUKE 2:4–7)**

THE CHURCH OF THE NATIVITY—considered the birthplace of Jesus—was built around AD 330 by the first Christian Roman emperor, Constantine. (Dominika Zara / Shutterstock.com)

BIBLE STUFF THAT HAPPENED IN BETHLEHEM

- Jacob's wife Rachel was buried in Bethlehem.
- Naomi's hometown and where Ruth met Boaz.
- Hometown of Jesse and his famous son David. This is where Samuel anointed David to be the king.
- A Philistine garrison was stationed here during David's reign. Three of David's soldiers broke through that defense and drew water from Bethlehem and returned it to David.
- Bethlehem, which was in the northern part of the land of Judah, became known as "the city of David."
- King Rehoboam of Judah fortified Bethlehem.
- People from Bethlehem are mentioned in two lists of Jews returning from the Babylonian captivity.
- The promise of a Messiah to be born in Bethlehem was given in Micah 5:2.
- Jesus is born here!

WHERE TO FIND IT IN ISRAEL

The ancient town of Bethlehem is five miles south of Jerusalem. It is located in the southern Judean mountains, and it has an elevation about one hundred feet higher than Jerusalem's. You can travel from Jerusalem to Bethlehem by tour bus.

THINGS TO SEE

◆ **The Church of the Nativity:** Built in the 500s, it contains what some contend is the actual birthplace of Jesus and is one of the oldest Christian churches anywhere. The supposed spot where Jesus was born is marked by a silver star. The Church of the Nativity is a UNESCO World Heritage site.

◆ **Rachel's Tomb:** This is considered a holy site by all three monotheistic religions: Christians, Jews, and Muslims. It is under Israeli control.

◆ **The Shepherds' Field:** A number of places vie for designation of the one true field where the shepherds heard the announcement of Jesus's birth—but even if we don't know for sure, the places still evoke the awe of that historic pronouncement.

◆ **Solomon's Pools:** Some say this is the site from which Solomon wrote the Song of Songs.

◆ **David's Well:** Discovered in the late 1800s, this well could have been the water source David's soldiers used after he pined for water from Bethlehem (SEE 2 SAMUEL 23:15–17).

Gary Hardman / Freeimages.com

FAVORITE SITE REFLECTION

Entering **the opening** that leads to what is considered the traditional site of Jesus's birth is a little tricky. Here you are at one of the most hallowed locations in Christian history, and visitors have to duck into a passageway that is about four feet high. But why not bow? It seemed to me to be a reminder that the first people who visited Jesus at the site of His birth probably bowed down as well—the shepherds. Once inside, you don't get the feeling that this was a stable, but it seems more like a cave. Nonetheless, there is a true feeling of awe to consider being in a space, perhaps *the* space, where our Savior was born.

BETHSAIDA

*Immediately Jesus made his disciples get into the boat and go on ahead of him to **Bethsaida**, while he dismissed the crowd. After leaving them, he went up on a mountainside to pray.* **MARK 6:45–46**

BETHSAIDA: The ruins of the ancient city of Bethsaida in the Golan Heights. This gate dates back to the rule of David. On the right is a cultic stele depicting a Canaanite deity. (Mboesch / Creative Commons)

WHERE TO FIND IT IN THE BIBLE

Matthew 11:21;
Mark 6:45; 8:22;
Luke 9:10; 10:13;
John 1:44; 12:21

KEY PASSAGES ABOUT BETHSAIDA

❝ Woe to you, Bethsaida! . . . I tell you, it will be more bearable for Tyre and Sidon on the day of judgment than for you. **(MATTHEW 11:21–22)**

❝ The next day Jesus decided to leave for Galilee. Finding Philip, he said to him, "Follow me." Philip, like Andrew and

Peter, was from the town of Bethsaida. (JOHN 1:43–44)

BIBLE STUFF THAT HAPPENED IN BETHSAIDA

● Bethsaida was the hometown of Philip, Andrew, and Peter.

● Jesus was on a mountainside near Bethsaida when He walked out on the waters of the Sea of Galilee to rescue the disciples, who were struggling with their boat because of rough water and high winds.

● It was at Bethsaida that Jesus healed a blind man with a two-part healing.

● At Bethsaida, Jesus fed the five thousand.

● Jesus pronounced a curse on Bethsaida.

WHERE TO FIND IT IN ISRAEL

Bethsaida is located at the northern tip of the Sea of Galilee, not far to the east of Capernaum.

Like many other biblical sites, there is some controversy about where the biblical city is located. One group of researchers had pinpointed Tel-Bethsaida, which is inland a bit from the Sea of Galilee. Those who support this as the town's location say that geological changes over the past two thousand years have separated the sea and the town. This site is reached by turning north on Route 888 from Route 87, which lies just north of the Sea of Galilee. Visitors wishing to see this archaeological site will go to a place called Yarden Park. It contains not just the ruins but also other entertainment options.

The second candidate is el-Araj, which is closer to the current-day Sea of Galilee. Supporters of this location feel that this Roman-built city was the one on the coast of the Sea.

To see el-Araj, visitors will go to the Bethsaida Valley Nature Reserve.

Visit both, and you can decide for yourself.

Ruins of a fishing village, perhaps Bethsaida mentioned in John 1. If so, it is where fishermen Peter, James, and John once lived. (Chmee2 / Creative Commons)

CAESAREA BY

*When the cavalry arrived in **Caesarea**, they delivered the letter to the governor and handed Paul over to him.*

ACTS 23:33

CAESAREA BY THE SEA: Long ago abandoned as a residence, Caesarea still offers a number of fascinating ruins suggestive of its heyday. The area that was left behind is now part of Caesarea National Park. (Terry Bidgood / ODBM)

THE SEA

WHERE TO FIND IT IN THE BIBLE

Acts 8:40; 9:30; 10:1, 24; 12:19; 18:22; 21:8, 16; 23:23, 33; 24:1; 25:1, 4, 6, 13, 24

KEY PASSAGES ABOUT CAESAREA BY THE SEA

❝ When the believers learned of this [that some wanted to kill Paul], they took him down to Caesarea and sent him off to Tarsus. **(ACTS 9:30)**

❝ At Caesarea there was a man named Cornelius, a centurion

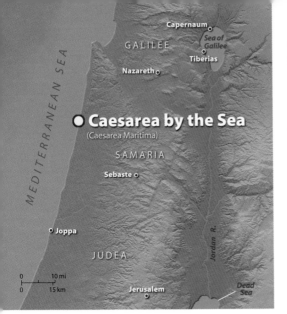

they brought their charges against Paul before the governor. (ACTS 24:1)

BIBLE STUFF THAT HAPPENED IN CAESAREA

A number of significant biblical events occurred in Caesarea, a city built by Herod the Great. The city became the capital of Judea, and it was home to both Herod and a number of top officials. It was the seat of Roman power in Israel.

● A Roman centurion named Cornelius was called by God to have some men get Peter. When Peter came to Caesarea, he preached the gospel to Cornelius and others, and several trusted Jesus Christ as Savior.

● It was at Caesarea by the Sea that Paul stood before Festus to answer to charges brought against him. As a result of this trial, Paul was sent to Rome to be tried.

WHERE TO FIND IT IN ISRAEL

Caesarea by the Sea is located on the Mediterranean Sea on the north coast of Israel. It is about an hour south of Haifa and about an hour north of Tel Aviv. It is about seventy miles northwest of Jerusalem.

THINGS TO SEE

◆ One of the most fascinating ancient sites to see in Caesarea is an *elevated*

in what was known as the Italian Regiment. [He was called by God to go get Peter.] (ACTS 10:1)

❝ Then Herod went from Judea to Caesarea and stayed there. (ACTS 12:19)

❝ When [Paul] landed at Caesarea, he went up to Jerusalem and greeted the church and then went down to Antioch. (ACTS 18:22)

❝ Five days later the high priest Ananias went down to Caesarea with some of the elders and a lawyer named Tertullus, and

aqueduct that was built around a hundred years after Christ. It was built to transfer water about sixteen kilometers from some springs down to Caesarea.

◆ Also, a **Roman theater** by the ocean makes it easy to imagine yourself sitting in the stone seats and watching a play. The theater was built in the first century AD. In fact, a visitor doesn't have to imagine. The amphitheater has been restored so that concerts are held there in the summer.

◆ Other ruins that can be found: A series of buildings, which probably contains the **home of Pontius Pilate**. A **hippodrome**, the location of entertainment such as chariot races in ancient Caesarea. Recent excavations reveal what experts suspect was **Herod's Palace**. Visitors can see pillars at this site that may have been in existence when Paul was on trial in that city.

FAVORITE SITE REFLECTION

Infrastructure is probably not a word that would draw most people's attention if they were thinking of reasons why a historical location appeals to them. But I am fascinated with how a civilization makes life work in its locale. In many parts of the world, for

Terry Bidgood / ODBM

instance, getting water to the citizens is still difficult. Now think back thousands of years and imagine how hard it was to supply this life-giving substance. In Caesarea by the Sea, that problem was solved with the construction of an **aqueduct**. It was built under the leadership of Herod, taking water from a spring sixteen miles away and letting it run to Caesarea, which had little fresh water. Visiting this city, seeing this

magnificent arched structure, and imagining that it ran for sixteen miles is a highlight for anyone who marvels at the ingenuity of what we consider ancient civilizations.

6

CAESAREA PHILIPPI

**HERMON STREAM (Banias)
NATURE RESERVE**—with its lush
vegetation and breathtaking
waterfalls—features the ruins of a
temple devoted to the god Paneas
(Banias in Arabic), commonly referred
to as Pan. (Gugganij / Creative Commons)

*When Jesus came to the region of **Caesarea
Philippi,** he asked his disciples, "Who do
people say the Son of Man is?"* MATTHEW 16:13

WHERE TO FIND IT IN THE BIBLE

Matthew 16:13;
Mark 8:27

KEY PASSAGE ABOUT CAESAREA PHILIPPI

❝ Jesus and his disciples went on to the villages around Caesarea Philippi. On the way he asked them, "Who do people say I am?" **(MARK 8:27)**

Caesarea Philippi

Question on identity leads to Peter's confession

Tyre

Capernaum

Gergesa

GALILEE

Sea of Galilee

Sepphoris

Nazareth

DECAPOLIS

BIBLE STUFF THAT HAPPENED IN CAESAREA PHILIPPI

● While the Bible records only one incident that took place at Caesarea Philippi, the location has enduring influence and interest. The location itself is fascinating because of the cultural implications that are connected to it. And it is biblically important because of key statements made by Peter and by Jesus at Caesarea Philippi.

● Matthew, Mark, and Luke—all three— record the vital meeting that took place between Jesus and His disciples at this northernmost location of Jesus's ministry. Jesus turned to His disciples and asked them, "Who do people say the Son of Man is?"

● Peter responded with an earthshaking truth: "You are the Messiah, the Son of the living God." And Jesus replied, "On this rock I will build my church, and the gates of Hades will not overcome it" **(MATTHEW 16:16, 18).**

● The cultural significance of the location is fascinating, for one reason, because it was a pagan worship center. One geographic landmark of the area was a huge cave that seemed carved out of the foothills of Mount Hermon. It was referred to as "the gate of Hell," which may very well have been used by Jesus as a gaping object lesson as He talked to His disciples.

WHERE TO FIND IT IN ISRAEL

The location of this amazing exchange is referred to as Hermon Stream (Banias) Nature Reserve. *Fodor's Essential Israel* describes it this way: "One of the most stunning parts of Israel, this reserve contains gushing waterfalls, dense foliage along riverbanks, and the remains of a temple dedicated to the god Pan."[4]

The trip from Jerusalem to Hermon Stream (Banias) Nature Reserve takes around three hours, depending on the route.

THINGS TO SEE

The site no longer boasts the pagan idols or the cult worship buildings of the first century, but it is not hard to imagine them while looking at the rocky surroundings of what is called **Banias**. The cave is still there, and one can see holes in the rocks where idols such as Pan were once displayed. The location is beautiful because of the flowing waters and the rocky terrain. And what can be better than standing where Jesus and His disciples stood?

FAVORITE SITE REFLECTION

Perhaps it was the pure, natural beauty that drew me in at Caesarea Philippi. There was the lush growth of the trees and other greenery that was watered by the refreshing streams that came from the foothills of Mount Hermon. But once I was there, surrounded by the magnificence of this natural phenomenon, I began to grow more influenced by what I was hearing. Standing below the rocky face of **an outcropping that led to Mount Hermon**, we listened spellbound as our guide explained the contrast between the Canaanite paganism of the area and the pure gospel that Jesus had brought His disciples here to examine. Seeing this setting for Jesus's essential discussion with His followers about who He is brought the Matthew 16:13–20 passage into a reality that I have never forgotten.

Terry Bidgood / ODBM

CAPERNAUM

7

THE SYNAGOGUE RUINS in the town of Capernaum have tremendous significance. While the upper-level remains are left over from the fourth century, it is believed that the foundation and the floor that tourists can walk on were in existence in Jesus's day. (Terry Bidgood / ODBM)

*They went to **Capernaum**, and when the Sabbath came, Jesus went into the synagogue and began to teach.*

MARK 1:21

WHERE TO FIND IT IN THE BIBLE

Matthew 4:13; 8:5; 11:23; 17:24; Mark 1:21; 2:1; 9:33; Luke 4:23; 4:31; 7:1; 10:15; John 2:12; 4:46; 6:17, 24, 59

KEY PASSAGES ABOUT CAPERNAUM

❝ Leaving Nazareth, [Jesus] went and lived in Capernaum, . . . to fulfill what was said through the prophet Isaiah. **(MATTHEW 4:13–14)**

> ❝ Then [Jesus] went down to Capernaum, a town in Galilee, and on the Sabbath he taught the people. They were amazed at his teaching, because his words had authority. **(LUKE 4:31–32)**

BIBLE STUFF THAT HAPPENED IN CAPERNAUM

● A centurion asked Jesus to help because his servant was paralyzed. The soldier had such strong faith in Jesus that He said, "Truly I tell you, I have not found anyone in Israel with such great faith." And Jesus healed the servant **(MATTHEW 8:5–13)**.

● Jesus warned the people of Capernaum

about rejecting His words **(LUKE 10:15)**.

● Jesus demonstrated the importance of paying the temple tax by having Peter find a coin in a fish with which to pay the tax **(MATTHEW 17:24–27)**.

● Jesus drove out a demon. The demon had identified Jesus as the "Holy One of God" **(LUKE 4:31–35)**.

● Jesus healed a paralyzed man who had been lowered through the roof of the home they were in **(MARK 2:1–5)**. Jesus forgave the man's sins, which caused some of the teachers to suggest Jesus was blasphemous **(MARK 2:6–7)**.

WHERE TO FIND IT IN ISRAEL

Capernaum is one of many Jesus-era towns that are found in various locations on the shore of the Sea of Galilee. Today, Route 87 runs along the western coast of the Sea heading north out of Tiberias. Capernaum is near the northernmost tip of the Sea of Galilee. The town where Jesus made His home during His ministry is about eighty-five miles from Jerusalem.

THINGS TO SEE

◆ Upon entering Capernaum, visitors see *a sign that reads: "Capernaum: Hometown of Jesus."* This can be surprising at first, because Nazareth usually gets that designation. But this town became Jesus's home away from home during His ministry.

◆ **The synagogue ruins** that highlight the town of Capernaum have tremendous significance. While the upper-level remains are left over from the fourth century, it is believed that the foundation and the floor that tourists can walk on were in existence in Jesus's day. Christ, in all probability, was teaching from that location in the story recorded in Mark 1. It was this synagogue that was purchased and built with the help of the centurion mentioned in Luke 7. It is truly amazing to visit this synagogue with those facts in mind.

◆ Within the site of the synagogue are ruins covered by a modern-looking roof structure. The ruins are **the home of Peter's mother-in-law.** In three of the gospels, the story of Jesus healing her is mentioned—and it took place in that home in Capernaum.

FAVORITE SITE REFLECTION

It doesn't take long to feel the power of this little town. There is not much left from the first century, but what is there shouts its importance. Imagine walking on the same stone foundation of the synagogue that hosted Jesus! Inside walls similar to the ones still there, our Savior taught in such a way that the people were amazed. It is not difficult to picture Him in that location, mesmerizing the people with His knowledge and wisdom. And inside this small stone building, Jesus cast out demons. Jesus walked and preached where we stand today as visitors!

James Emery / Creative Commons

As I took it all in, I looked toward the Sea of Galilee—just yards away, it seems—and there was the house—**the very house—where Jesus healed Peter's mother-in-law.**

How awesome it was to feel the power of being in "the town of Jesus."

The Danites rebuilt the city and settled there. They named it **Dan** *after their ancestor Dan, who was born to Israel— though the city used to be called Laish.*

JUDGES 18:28–29

8

DAN

WHERE TO FIND IT IN THE BIBLE

Genesis 14:14; Numbers 2:25; Deuteronomy 34:1;
Joshua 19:47; Judges 18:29; 20:1; 1 Samuel 3:20;
2 Samuel 3:10; 17:11; 24:2, 15; 1 Kings 4:25; 12:30; 15:20;
2 Chronicles 2:14; 30:5; Jeremiah 4:15; Ezekiel 48

KEY PASSAGE ABOUT DAN

❝ When the territory of the Danites was lost to them, they went up and attacked Leshem, took it, put it to the sword and occupied it. They

ABRAHAM'S GATE, the city's main gate located on the east side of Dan, was a triple-arch entrance made of sun-baked bricks (reconstructed by archaeologists). It is thought to have been in existence when Abraham went to Dan to try to find Lot.
(DinaKuzia / Creative Commons)

The **Dan Stream**, which eventually feeds into the Jordan River. (Valerossi / Pixabay.com)

settled in Leshem and named it Dan after their ancestor. **(JOSHUA 19:47)**

BIBLE STUFF THAT HAPPENED IN DAN

● Abram made his way to Dan when he went north with 318 trained men to try to find Lot, who had been abducted **(GENESIS 14:14).**

● Dan was used often as a descriptive geographic marker in the Bible to denote the northernmost point in Israel—paired with Beersheba as the southernmost point. We see this in numerous passages, including 1 Samuel 3:20, 2 Samuel 3:10,

1 Kings 4:25, and others. For instance: "And all Israel from Dan to Beersheba recognized that Samuel was attested as a prophet of the LORD."

● Dan was the main city in the territory given to the tribe of Dan. It is also referred to as Laish and Leshem **(JOSHUA 19:47 AND JUDGES 18:7).**

● One of the key craftsmen for Solomon's temple, Huram-Abi, had his maternal roots in Dan.

● When Rehoboam became king, he did not want the people to go to Jerusalem to worship, so he set up worship centers at Bethel and Dan. At these worship centers, he installed golden calves for the people to worship (**1 KINGS 12:29–33**).

● King Ben-Hadad conquered Dan, according to 1 Kings 15:20. The punishment of Jeroboam's idolatrous act was the destruction of Dan and defeat at the hands of the Assyrians.

WHERE TO FIND IT IN ISRAEL

Dan is located at the northern extreme of Israel, not far from Mount Hermon and in a region called the Huleh Basin. Therefore, it is near the headwaters of the Jordan River. Dan is situated very near the border with Syria. Dan is about twenty-five miles north of the Sea of Galilee.

To get to Dan, you take Highway 90 north. At Highway 99, turn east before arriving at the tel. The trip from Jerusalem to Dan takes approximately three hours. Along with the tel, there is a nature preserve at Dan, so it is a great place for hiking and enjoying the headwaters of the Jordan.

Oren Rozen / Creative Commons

THINGS TO SEE

◆ **Tel Dan:** An archaeological dig at the site of the ancient city. Archaeologists have been digging through the ancient remains since the 1960s. Among the items that have been unearthed: A rock wall that has been dated to the time of Solomon's temple. Researchers perceive it to be part of an entrance built by King Ahab to protect the city. Also, a structure referred to as **Abraham's Gate** has been unearthed. It is said to be four thousand years old, and it may have been in existence when Abraham went to Dan to try to find Lot (**GENESIS 14:14**).

◆ Another remarkable important archaeological site to visit is the **High Place of Jeroboam,** which would have been the temple in which Jeroboam kept the golden calves he wanted the people to worship.

◆ Also at Tel Dan **an ancient basalt stele** (stone slab) was discovered in the 1990s. On this stele is the mention of a victory over the "House of David," inscribed in Aramaic. This important find is the only time King David's role has been mentioned in any extra-biblical findings. The stele is not at Dan; it is on display at the Israel Museum in Jerusalem.

DEAD SEA

9

Your southern side will include some of the Desert of Zin along the border of Edom. Your southern boundary will start in the east from the southern end of the **Dead Sea.** NUMBERS 34:3

THE DEAD SEA's surface is 1,412 feet below sea level, the lowest elevation of land on Earth. It is 9.6 times saltier than the ocean. Its mineral content, reduced ultraviolet radiation, and higher atmospheric pressure make the Dead Sea a focus for various health treatments. (Terry Bidgood / ODBM)

WHERE TO FIND IT IN THE BIBLE

Genesis 14:3: Numbers 34:3, 12; Deuteronomy 3:17; 4:49; Joshua 3:16; 12:3; 2 Kings 14:25; Ezekiel 47:8; Joel 2:20

KEY PASSAGES ABOUT THE DEAD SEA

❝ All these latter kings joined forces in the Valley of Siddim

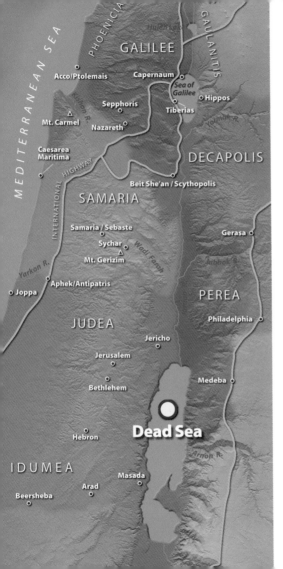

The Dead Sea is centrally located near a number of biblical sites, including (top) Masada (Terry Bidgood / OD and (right) the caves of Qumran where the Dead Se Scrolls were discovered (Juha67 / Pixabay.com).

(that is, the Dead Sea Valley). **(GENESIS 14:3)**

❝ The water from upstream stopped flowing. It piled up in a heap a great distance away, at a town called Adam in the vicinity of Zarethan, while the water flowing down to the Sea of the Arabah (that is, the Dead Sea) was completely cut off. **(JOSHUA 3:16)**

❝ Then the boundary will go down along the Jordan and end at the Dead Sea. "This will be your land, with its boundaries on every side." **(NUMBERS 34:12)**

> **"** This water flows toward the eastern region and goes down into the Arabah, where it enters the Dead Sea. When it empties into the sea, the salty water there becomes fresh. **(EZEKIEL 47:8)**

BIBLE STUFF THAT HAPPENED AT THE DEAD SEA

● Unlike the Sea of Galilee, the waters of the Dead Sea are not the location of Bible events. We don't read of people sailing across it or fishing in it. Instead, we see this huge body of water as a boundary marker in many instances and as a key element of future changes.

What we do see is a number of key areas in the vicinity of the Dead Sea as being important, both in the Bible and in the history of the Bible itself as a book. For instance, **the oasis of En Gedi** is close to the Dead Sea, as were the cities of **Sodom and Gomorrah**.

WHERE TO FIND IT IN ISRAEL

The northern tip of the Dead Sea is about twenty miles east of Jerusalem. The Sea then extends to the south for about thirty miles. At the lower end of the Dead Sea is the Negev Desert. The border between Israel and Jordan runs roughly through the middle of the Dead Sea.

THINGS TO SEE

◆ Perhaps the most famous site near the Dead Sea is **Qumran**, where the Dead Sea Scrolls were discovered in the 1940s. This was the home of the Essenes in the first century AD. It was this people group who preserved Scripture in clay jars that were discovered by accident in area caves in 1947. A visit to Qumran yields a more complete picture of the Essenes and a view of those caves.

◆ **Masada:** This famous plateau overlooks the Dead Sea in its southern portion. It was a hilltop location fortified by King Herod. Later, it became a Jewish stronghold with a fascinating history. A cable car takes visitors to the top of Masada where amazing first-century ruins can be explored.

43

10

EN GEDI

The **EN GEDI** (now called **Ein Gedi)** oasis and nature reserve is just west of the Dead Sea on the eastern edge of the Judean Desert. (Yair Aronshtam / Shutterstock.com)

And David went up from [Sela Hammahlekoth] and lived in the strongholds of **En Gedi.** 1 SAMUEL 23:29

WHERE TO FIND IT IN THE BIBLE

Joshua 15:62; 1 Samuel 23:29; 24:1; 2 Chronicles 20:2; Song of Songs 1:14; Ezekiel 47:10

KEY PASSAGES ABOUT EN GEDI

❝ After Saul returned from pursuing the Philistines, he was told, "David is in the Desert of En Gedi." **(1 SAMUEL 24:1)**

❝ Some people came and told Jehoshaphat, "A vast army is coming against you from Edom, from the other side of the Dead Sea. It is already in Hazezon Tamar" (that is, En Gedi). **(2 CHRONICLES 20:2)**

❝ My beloved is to me a cluster of henna blossoms from the vineyards of En Gedi. **(SONG OF SONGS 1:14)**

45

BIBLE STUFF THAT HAPPENED AT EN GEDI

- In the book of Joshua, En Gedi was mentioned as a town in the desert given to the tribe of Judah when the Promised Land was distributed to the tribes.
- Saul was closing in on David in the Desert of Maon, but a messenger told Saul that the Philistines were "raiding the land" (1 SAMUEL 23:27). Saul stopped pursuing David at that time. David then went to the "strongholds of En Gedi" to stay for a while (1 SAMUEL 23:29). King Saul sent three thousand men after David in the En Gedi region. In this region David spoke to Saul, and Saul stopped his pursuit of him.
- An army that was threatening King Jehoshaphat reached En Gedi as it made its way to attack him.
- The "beloved" of Song of Songs was compared with the blossoms from vineyards at En Gedi.

WHERE TO FIND IT IN ISRAEL

En Gedi, which is a large oasis on the west side of the Dead Sea, is located southeast of Jerusalem. The driving time from Jerusalem to En Gedi is about an hour and twenty minutes.

THINGS TO SEE

◆ *En Gedi Nature Reserve:* The area of En Gedi is now a nature preserve that is a definite relief from the surrounding desert. Natural springs water the location, and the waterfall of En Gedi is a beautiful highlight. Also, visitors can see Nahal David, containing a cave that some believe was one of David's hideouts

Ester Inbar / Creative Commons

Yuvalr / Creative Commons

over a thousand years. A visit to the En Gedi Antiquities National Park will add to the knowledge of the area's history.

EN GEDI TODAY

A botanical garden was built by the people of present-day En Gedi, and it contains nearly a thousand species of plants from around the world. A traveler can easily take a bus from Jerusalem to En Gedi. Because of its proximity to the Dead Sea, a visitor can also swim in that unusual body of water on the trip to En Gedi.

FAVORITE SITE REFLECTION

Somewhat like Caesarea Philippi, En Gedi evokes both the majesty of God's beautiful creation and the excitement of being where an important story from biblical history took place. En Gedi stands in stark contrast to its surroundings because it is an oasis in the wilderness. The beauty of waterfall, vegetation, and an occasional **ibex** bring a pleasant surprise to tourists who come expecting just ruins and ancient shrines. But that can't match the excitement of thinking you just might be looking at the cave where David sneaked in on Saul and snipped off a piece of his robe.

while keeping away from King Saul.

◆ *Caves:* A visit to En Gedi also brings you up close to the many caves, which gave David places to hide from Saul.

◆ Hiking visitors can explore the area to enjoy the fascinating flora and fauna.

◆ *Archaeological excavation:* An ancient synagogue has been excavated on this site, and its mosaic floor can be seen. En Gedi was a continuous Jewish habitation for

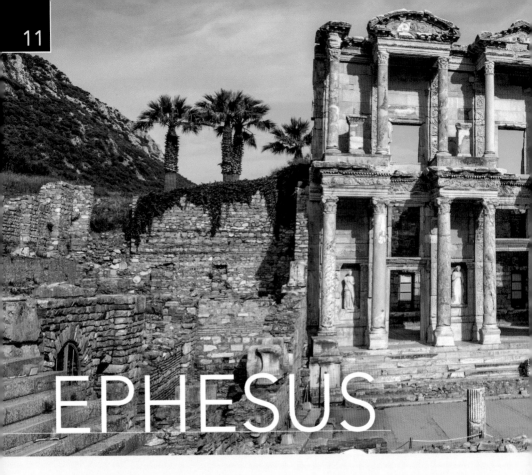

11

EPHESUS

*They arrived at **Ephesus,** where Paul left Priscilla and Aquila. He himself went into the synagogue and reasoned with the Jews.* ACTS 18:19

THE **LIBRARY OF CELSUS** in Ephesus, built around AD 117, was a monumental tomb for Gaius Julius Celsus Polemaeanus, the governor of the province. Celsus's grave was beneath the ground floor. With a capacity of more than 12,000 scrolls, Celsus was the third-largest library in the Roman world. It is one of the only remaining examples of a library from the Roman Empire. (Alex Soh / ODBM)

WHERE TO FIND IT IN THE BIBLE

Acts 18:19, 21, 24; 19:1, 17, 26, 35; 20:16–17;
1 Corinthians 15:32; 16:8; Ephesians 1:1; 1 Timothy 1:3;
2 Timothy 1:18; 4:12; Revelation 1:11, 2:1

KEY PASSAGES ABOUT EPHESUS

❝ Paul, an apostle of Christ
Jesus by the will of God, to God's

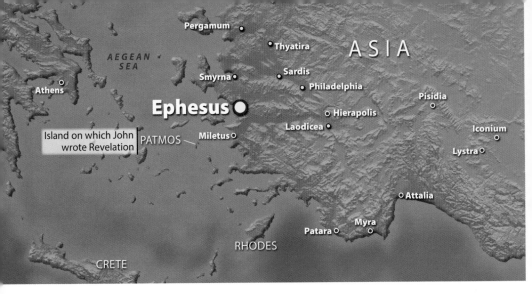

AEGEAN SEA

Pergamum

Thyatira

ASIA

Athens

Smyrna

Sardis

Philadelphia

Pisidia

Ephesus

Hierapolis

Laodicea

Island on which John wrote Revelation

PATMOS

Miletus

Iconium

Lystra

Attalia

Myra

Patara

RHODES

CRETE

holy people in Ephesus, the faithful in Christ Jesus. **(EPHESIANS 1:1)**

❝ To the angel of the church in Ephesus write: These are the words of him who holds the seven stars in his right hand and walks among the seven golden lampstands. **(REVELATION 2:1)**

BIBLE STUFF THAT HAPPENED AT EPHESUS

● After being in Corinth, Paul arrived in Ephesus and left his friends Priscilla and Aquila there **(ACTS 18:18–19)**. Paul also went to the synagogue to reason with the Jews **(v. 19)** before leaving for Caesarea.

● Paul was on his way to Jerusalem when he "took the road through the interior and arrived at Ephesus" **(ACTS 19:1)**. He stayed in Ephesus and for three months he spoke in the synagogue. Some listeners refused to believe, so he moved on to a lecture hall, where he preached for two years. "The word of the Lord spread widely" **(v. 20)**. Toward the end of his stay, there was a major uproar in Ephesus because the people who made shrines of Artemis were afraid they would lose business because of Paul's teachings.

● Paul wrote his letter to the church in Ephesus while he was in prison in Rome.

● Paul wrote to Timothy, who was

preaching in Ephesus, telling him not to let certain false teachers continue to teach.

● The apostle John probably lived in Ephesus near the end of his life. One of the letters to the seven churches that John wrote was addressed to the church at Ephesus.

WHERE TO FIND IT IN TURKEY

The ruins of the ancient city of Ephesus are found near the western border of Turkey, about ten miles from a place call Selçuk. Bus service to Ephesus is available.

THINGS TO SEE

"Archaeologists have worked at Ephesus for more than a century. These intense efforts have resulted in the excavation of nearly 15 percent of the ancient city."[5]

◆ One of the seven wonders of the ancient world once stood watch over Ephesus. It was *the Temple of Artemis,* the goddess of nature (SEE ACTS 19:35). The building was destroyed in the third century. Its foundation is all that is left of it in Ephesus.

◆ A "paved" street called *Curetes Street* lined with ruins of old Ephesus is still in existence. Ceremonies to honor Artemis were held along this street.

◆ The ruins of the *Library of Celsus* can still be seen. Two stories of its façade remain standing. During the second century AD, it had some 12,000 scrolls.

ite of the **Temple of Artemis**—one of the Seven Wonders of the Ancient World—in the town of Selçuk, near Ephesus. (Adam Carr / Creative Commons)

Then Jesus went with his disciples to a place called **Gethsemane**, and he said to them, "Sit here while I go over there and pray." MATTHEW 26:36

12

GARDEN OF

WHERE TO FIND IT IN THE BIBLE

Matthew 26:36; Mark 14:32; Luke 22:39–46

KEY PASSAGE ABOUT THE GARDEN OF GETHSEMANE

❝ They went to a place called Gethsemane, and Jesus said to his disciples, "Sit here while I pray." **(MARK 14:32)**

Alex Soh / ODBM

GETHSEMANE

BIBLE STUFF THAT HAPPENED AT THE GARDEN

● Two of the key events in Jesus's life happened in this grove of olive trees known as the garden of Gethsemane. First, Jesus went to the garden after the Last Supper to pray. He asked His disciples Peter, James, and John to wait with Him while He prayed, but they fell asleep. While Jesus was praying, Luke records, an angel came to Jesus to strengthen Him (22:43). It was at this location that Jesus prayed with such passion that He sweat drops of blood.

● Jesus began to address His sleeping followers, telling them that they needed to pray so they would not fall into temptation. As He was talking to His followers, Judas and a group of others interrupted Jesus, and the wayward disciple kissed Jesus—signaling that it was Jesus they should arrest.

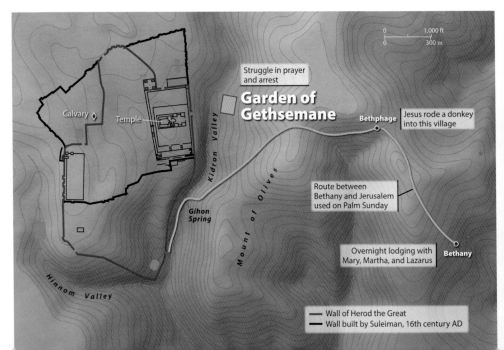

Struggle in prayer and arrest

Garden of Gethsemane

Calvary

Temple

Kidron Valley

Gihon Spring

Mount of Olives

Bethphage — Jesus rode a donkey into this village

Route between Bethany and Jerusalem used on Palm Sunday

Overnight lodging with Mary, Martha, and Lazarus — Bethany

Hinnom Valley

0 — 1,000 ft
0 — 300 m

— Wall of Herod the Great
— Wall built by Suleiman, 16th century AD

Terry Bidgood / ODBM

WHERE TO FIND IT IN ISRAEL

No trip to Jerusalem would be complete without a visit to the garden of Gethsemane. It is located at the foot of the Mount of Olives just across the Kidron Valley from the city of Jerusalem. Today, the garden itself is contained in a walled section of the grounds of the Church of All Nations.

THINGS TO SEE

The peaceful calm of the garden can still be felt to some degree, even though passing traffic nearby does remind the visitor that this is not the first century anymore.

The trees in the grove are assuredly not the same trees under which Jesus sat down to pray. Those were cut down a few decades later when Rome laid waste to the city of Jerusalem. Yet it is possible that these trees were descendants of some of those trees, for olive trees can stay alive for two thousand years.

While the view of the Temple Mount is obscured by trees and modernity, the view across the **Kidron Valley** is magnificent. One can imagine Jesus walking through one of the eastern gates after the Last Supper and heading to the garden.

55

13

GATH

*A champion named Goliath, who was from **Gath**, came out of the Philistine camp. His height was six cubits and a span.* **1 SAMUEL 17:4**

WHERE TO FIND IT IN THE BIBLE

Joshua 11:22; 13:3; 19:45; 21:24, 25; 1 Samuel 5:8; 6:17; 7:14; 17:4, 23, 52; 21:10, 12; 22:1; 27:2, 3, 4, 11; 2 Samuel 1:20; 15:18; 21:20, 22; 1 Kings 2:39, 40, 41; 2 Kings 12:17; 14:25; 1 Chronicles 6:69; 7:21; 8:13

KEY PASSAGES ABOUT GATH

❝ So they called together all the rulers of the Philistines and asked them, "What shall we do with the ark of the god of Israel?" They answered, "Have the ark of the god of Israel moved to Gath." So they moved the ark of the God of Israel. **(1 SAMUEL 5:8)**

TELL ES-SAFI is the site most favored as the location of Gath. It is an archaeological mound or tell also known as Tel Zafit in Hebrew and is located inside Tel Zafit National Park. (Ori~ / Creative Commons)

> Then the men of Israel and Judah surged forward with a shout and pursued the Philistines to the entrance of Gath and to the gates of Ekron. Their dead were strewn along the Shaaraim road to Gath and Ekron. **(1 SAMUEL 17:52)**

> That day David fled from Saul and went to Achish king of Gath. **(1 SAMUEL 21:10)**

BIBLE STUFF THAT HAPPENED AT GATH

- Gath is mentioned in Joshua 13:3 as one of the cities inhabited by Philistine rulers.
- Gath was ruled by King Achish during the first three kingdoms of Israel.
- Most notably, the giant David slew, Goliath, was from Gath.

WHERE TO FIND IT IN ISRAEL

The archaeological dig relating to the ancient city of Gath is contained in the Tel Tzafit National Park. It is located midway between Ashkelon (on the Mediterranean coast) and Jerusalem. Gath is about 55 kilometers from Jerusalem. There were five cities in the region that were often mentioned together in the Old Testament: Ekron, Ashkelon, Ashdod, Gaza, and Gath.

To get to Gath from Jerusalem, take Route 1 toward Tel Aviv. At Latrun Junction, get on Route 3 and go about 20 kilometers. Turn left onto Route 383 and go about 6 kilometers. Turn right toward Zafit Power Station. After about 300 meters, turn right and go till you see a sign to turn into the Tel Tzafit excavations.

Gath lies on the western edge of the **Valley of Elah**, where David slew Goliath (Terry Bigood / ODBM). *Right:* The archaeological mound **Tell as-Safi** (Bukvoed / Creative Commons).

trench, Maeir concluded, represented a siege system built around the city as mentioned in 2 Kings 12:17.

● A thorough examination of pottery, cooking utensils, jewelry, and other items puts the time of Gath's habitation

THINGS TO SEE

◆ *Tell es-Safi:* An olive press has been discovered at Tell es-Safi, located at Gath.

◆ *A city gate* that was found at the dig has been presumed to be the gate referred to in 1 Samuel 21:10–13.

GATH TODAY

Gath is nothing but an archaeological dig today. The last time the area was inhabited was prior to the Israeli War of Independence in 1948.

The dig, under the direction of Aren Maeir from Bar-Ilan University, began in 1996. Among the findings that prove the site is the city of Gath connected with David and Goliath are the following:

● Maeir "noticed a previously unknown man-made trench that circles the cite."[6] This

into the ninth century BC. Gath was a viable city before David's life, meaning the meeting of the armies of Israel and the Philistines is historically feasible.

● An ostracon that was unearthed in 2005 contains a name that appears very similar to the name "Goliath." While it may not actually be his name, the evidence is that "Tell es-Safi yields the right time, the right material data, and the right location" to make the Goliath story possible at Gath.[7]

14

GOL

The two supposed sites of Golgotha. *Above:* **Gordon's Calvary,** also referred to as Skull Hill due to two large sunken holes resembling the eyes of a skull (Footballkickit / Creative Commons). *Right:* **The Church of the Holy Sepulchre**

GOTHA

*They brought Jesus to the place called **Golgotha** (which means "the place of the skull").* MARK 15:22

WHERE TO FIND IT IN THE BIBLE

Matthew 27:33; Mark 15:22; John 19:17

KEY PASSAGES ABOUT GOLGOTHA

❝ They came to a place called Golgotha (which means "the place of the skull"). **(MATTHEW 27:33)**

❝ Carrying his own cross, he went out to the place of the Skull (which in Aramaic is called Golgotha). **(JOHN 19:17)**

BIBLE STUFF THAT HAPPENED AT GOLGOTHA

Only one recorded biblical event happened at Golgotha, and it is exceedingly important. It was on this hill outside Jerusalem that Jesus

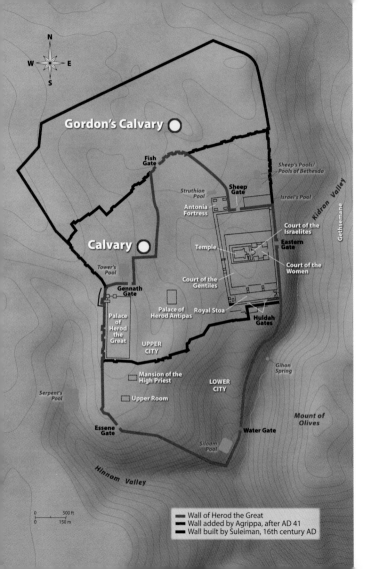

Map labels:

N W E S

Gordon's Calvary ○

Fish Gate

Sheep's Pools/ Pools of Bethesda

Struthion Pool

Sheep Gate

Antonia Fortress

Israel's Pool

Gethsemane

Kidron Valley

Calvary ○

Temple

Court of the Israelites

Eastern Gate

Court of the Women

Tower's Pool

Gennath Gate

Court of the Gentiles

Palace of Herod the Great

Palace of Herod Antipas

Royal Stoa

Huldah Gates

UPPER CITY

Gihon Spring

Mansion of the High Priest

LOWER CITY

Upper Room

Mount of Olives

Serpent's Pool

Essene Gate

Water Gate

Siloam Pool

Hinnom Valley

0   500 ft
0   150 m

Wall of Herod the Great
Wall added by Agrippa, after AD 41
Wall built by Suleiman, 16th century AD

---

allowed himself to be brutally murdered—crucified—as the perfect sacrifice for the sin of mankind.

It was on Jesus's way to the Place of the Skull that Simon (a man who was from Cyrene, which is modern-day Libya) was asked to carry the cross. Cyrene is located on Africa's north coast. It is possible that Simon was a black man. As Simon helped Jesus with the cross, they were followed toward Golgotha by a group of mourning and wailing women.

When Jesus arrived at the Place of the Skull, He was crucified between two criminals.

WHERE TO FIND IT IN ISRAEL

The exact location of Golgotha is a matter of intense discussion. Some say He was crucified at a site that is now covered by the Church of the Holy

Sepulchre. This location was approved in the fourth century by Helena, the mother of Roman emperor Constantine.[8] One difficulty with this site is that it is located inside Jerusalem's walls, which seems to contradict Hebrews 13:12, which indicates that Jesus suffered "outside the city gate." (See also Matthew 27:31, Mark 15:20.) However, some excavations of the site of the Church indicate that it is built where tombs once were located—and that would have had to have been outside the gates. Also, some historians refer to a northern wall that could have been inside the area of the Church.

A second possible spot is called Gordon's Calvary, named after General Charles Gordon, who in the 1880s found a site outside the walls that he said is the correct site.

So, the best tactic to take for someone visiting is to visit both the Church of the Holy Sepulchre and Gordon's Calvary. Both have elements that are fascinating and awe-inspiring.

The Church of the Holy Sepulchre is located in the Christian Quarter of the Old City. If a person were to enter the Old City at the Jaffa Gate on the west side, he or she could walk down David Street to Christian Quarter Road and arrive at the Church.

The Garden Tomb and Gordon's Calvary are just north of the Damascus Gate to the Old City, entailing a short walk up Nablus Road to Conrad Schick Street.

THINGS TO SEE

◆ *Gordon's Calvary:* This has been a popular destination for Anglicans and Protestants. It is an outside location, and worship services are held at the Garden Tomb. A Good Friday service at this location is an amazingly worshipful event. There is no charge for admission to the Garden Tomb. Skull Hill, which many believe is Golgotha, can be seen from the Garden Tomb area.

◆ *Church of the Holy Sepulchre:* Inside this building, according to some, are both the site of Jesus's crucifixion and the site of His burial. Testing in 2016 on the materials at the tomb area confirm that the area could have been enshrined as Jesus's tomb in the 300s as some historical records contend. The purported site of Golgotha is enclosed in glass at this site. Parts of the building have been at this location for 1,700 years or so. A trip through the Church of the Holy Sepulchre can be demanding because of the crowds and the obvious religious veneration of many visiting what they consider the holiest site on Earth.

15

As for the other events of **Hezekiah's** *reign, all his achievements and how he made the pool and the* **tunnel** *by which he brought water into the city, are they not written in the book of the annals of the kings of Judah?* **2 KINGS 20:20**

HEZEK

WHERE TO FIND IT IN THE BIBLE

2 Kings 20:20; 2 Chronicles 32:30

KEY PASSAGES ABOUT HEZEKIAH'S TUNNEL

❝ As for the other events of Hezekiah's reign, all his achievements and how he made the pool and the tunnel by which he brought water into the city, are they not written in the book of the annals of the kings of Judah? **(2 KINGS 20:20)**

❝ It was Hezekiah who blocked the upper outlet of the Gihon spring and

Terry Bidgood / ODBM

channeled the water down to the west side of the City of David. (2 CHRONICLES 32:30)

BIBLE STUFF THAT HAPPENED AT HEZEKIAH'S TUNNEL

The biblical record mentions that Hezekiah was responsible for a pool and a tunnel, so there doesn't seem like much to go on. But history and archaeology have

Descending into **Hezekiah's Tunnel**—a water chann cut through bedrock beneath the City of David—at Gihon Spring end of the tunnel. (Ian Scott / Creative Comm

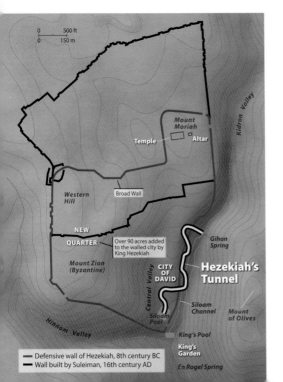

filled in the details of the fascinating story of Hezekiah's tunnel. First discovered in the modern era back in 1625, the tunnel was not attributed to Hezekiah until the late 1800s. The clincher was a stone sign that was found inside the tunnel. It explains that two teams of workers tunneled toward each other—and eventually met. This tablet is housed in the Istanbul Archaeology Museum.

Hezekiah's Tunnel was designed to take water from the Gihon Spring outside the city walls inside the city to the Pool of Siloam. The tunnel was a quarter of a mile long. The importance of the tunnel was to make sure that in case of siege by an enemy attacker, the city would not run dry. This was exactly what happened when the Assyrians attacked **(SEE 2 CHRONICLES 32:30)**.

Wikikati / Public domain

WHERE TO FIND IT IN JERUSALEM

Leaving the walled city through the Dung Gate, take Wadi Hilwa to the right until you arrive at the visitors' center of the City of David National Park. It is possible to walk through Hezekiah's Tunnel, but it is suggested that you wear shorts or swimming clothes and water shoes. Some wading will take place! Also, take along a flashlight. The tunnel is dark and narrow. You will be able to tour both the Tunnel and the Pool of Siloam. The Tunnel walk takes from twenty to forty minutes.

THINGS TO SEE

◆ *Gihon Spring:* This is the water source for Hezekiah's Tunnel. At one time this spring was used for irrigation in the Kidron Valley. But Hezekiah's Tunnel channeled the water a different direction.

◆ *Hezekiah's Tunnel:* This architectural wonder was dug with workmen starting at opposite ends and digging toward each other.

◆ *Pool of Siloam:* This pool was cut out of the rock to form a catch basin for the water that ran from Gihon Springs through Hezekiah's Tunnel. A visitor can visit the pool itself or trek through the tunnel to the pool.

◆ *Shiloh Inscription:* The original is in the Istanbul Archaeology Museum. But a visitor to the Hezekiah Tunnel can see **a facsimile** about six meters from the end of the tunnel. It was written in Hebrew, and it describes the moment when diggers from the springs met diggers from the Pool of Siloam to complete the tunnel.

16

JAFFA *or* JOPPA (TEL-AVIV)

We will cut all the logs from Lebanon that you need and will float them as rafts by sea down to **Joppa.** **2 CHRONICLES 2:16**

The Port of **Jaffa**, with Tel Aviv in the background. (Noam.armonn / Creative Commons)

WHERE TO FIND IT IN THE BIBLE

Joshua 19:46; 2 Chronicles 2:16; Ezra 3:7; Jonah 1:3; Acts 9:36, 38, 42, 43; 10:5, 8, 23; 11:5, 13

KEY PASSAGES ABOUT JAFFA/JOPPA

66 We will cut all the logs from Lebanon that you need and will float them as rafts

by sea down to Joppa. You can then take them to Jerusalem. **(2 CHRONICLES 2:16, BUILDING THE FIRST TEMPLE)**

❝ They gave money to the masons and carpenters, and gave food and drink and olive oil to the people of Sidon and Tyre, so that they would bring cedar logs by sea from Lebanon to Joppa, as authorized by Cyrus king of Persia. **(EZRA 3:7, BUILDING THE SECOND TEMPLE)**

❝ But Jonah ran away from the LORD and headed for Tarshish. He went down to Joppa, where he found a ship bound for that port. **(JONAH 1:3)**

❝ Peter stayed in Joppa for some time with a tanner named Simon. **(ACTS 9:43)**

BIBLE STUFF THAT HAPPENED IN JAFFA/JOPPA

● Joppa was used as a land marker to represent the western edge of the land of the tribe of Dan. Their territory faced Joppa.
● Twice Joppa is mentioned as the port of entry for cedar logs harvested in Lebanon, brought down the eastern edge of the

above: This home in the Old City of Jaffa is the supposed house of **Simon the Tanner**, where Peter stayed during the early days of Christian faith (Yoshi Canopus / Creative Commons). *Left:* The **Church of St. Peter**, purported site of Peter's vision in Acts (Berthold Werner / public domain).

Mediterranean, and taken ashore at Joppa.

● Joppa was the port of exit for Jonah as he headed west toward Tarshish instead of east toward Nineveh.

● The dressmaker Dorcas, whom Peter raised from the dead, lived in Joppa. Peter stayed awhile in Joppa after performing that miracle.

WHERE TO FIND IT IN ISRAEL

For travelers from the West visiting Israel via air, they won't miss Joppa. It is surrounded today by Tel-Aviv. And Tel-Aviv is the city where El Al and other air carriers land when taking tourists to Israel. Joppa is also called Jaffa. Jaffa is still the name of the harbor—representing the place from which Jonah set sail and where the cedars of Lebanon came ashore.

THINGS TO SEE

◆ After Peter raised Dorcas from the dead in Jaffa and continued on in the town, he later received a vision about animals on a large sheet (**ACTS 9:43–10:23**). That vision is remembered in Jaffa today at the Church of St. Peter, which purports to be on the location of Peter's vision.

◆ There is a home in Jaffa that is noted as the traditional site of Simon the Tanner (**ACTS 10:6**). Scripture says the house "is by the sea." The traditional site is indeed very close to the harbor.

◆ The Jaffa Port, which is located in the southern coast of Tel Aviv.[17]

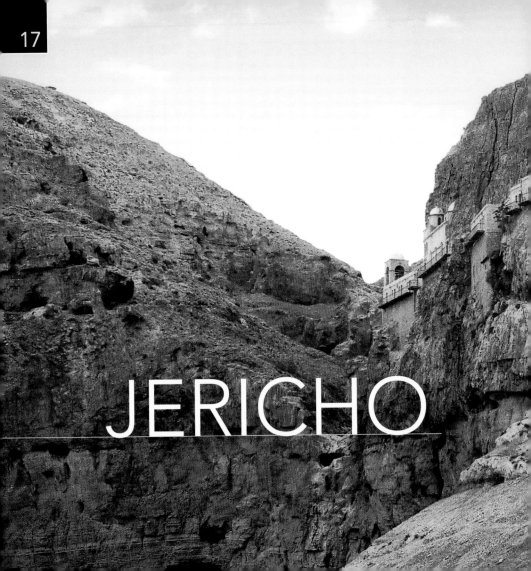

17

JERICHO

The MOUNT OF TEMPTATION, thought by some to be where Jesus was tempted by Satan, overlooks the city of Jericho. On its slopes today is the Monastery of Temptation, a Greek Orthodox monastery. (Gareththeobalditfyou / Pixabay.com)

*The LORD said to Joshua, "See, I have delivered **Jericho** into your hands, along with its king and its fighting men."*

JOSHUA 6:2

WHERE TO FIND IT IN THE BIBLE

Numbers 26:3, 63; 33:48, 50; 34:15; 35:1; Deuteronomy 32:49; 34:1, 3; Joshua 2:1–3; 3:16; 4:13, 19; 5:10, 13; 6:1, 2, 25–26; 7:2; 16:1, 7; 18:12, 21; 2 Kings 25:5; 2 Chronicles 28:15; Nehemiah 3:2; Matthew 20:29; Luke 10:30

KEY PASSAGES ABOUT JERICHO

❝ Moses climbed Mount Nebo from the plains of Moab to the top of Pisgah, across from Jericho. Then the LORD showed him the whole land—from Gilead to Dan. **(DEUTERONOMY 34:1)**

❝ Joshua son of Nun secretly sent two spies from Shittim. "Go, look over

the land," he said, "especially Jericho."
(JOSHUA 2:1)

❝ The king of Jericho sent this message to Rahab: "Bring out the men who came to you and entered your house, because they have come to spy out the whole land." But the woman had taken the two men and hidden them. (JOSHUA 2:3–4)

❝ Then the LORD said to Joshua, "See, I have delivered Jericho into your hands, along with its king and its fighting men." (JOSHUA 6:2)

❝ But Joshua spared Rahab. (JOSHUA 6:25)

❝ The allotment for Joseph began at the Jordan, east of the springs of Jericho, and went up from there through the desert into the hill country of Bethel. (JOSHUA 16:1)

❝ [Elijah and Elisha] went to Jericho. (2 KINGS 2:4)

BIBLE STUFF THAT HAPPENED IN JERICHO

● Jericho played a key role at the end of the wilderness period and the beginning of the Promised Land era for Israel. Spies were sent to scope out the city, and later God directed the Israelites to attack and destroy Jericho. This was the first battle the Israelites would have to face as they began to conquer the land God was giving them. Following God's instructions, Joshua led the Israelites to capture the city in an unusual way—by walking around it seven times.

● Rahab, called a "prostitute" in Joshua 6:25, helped the Israelites to defeat the city of Jericho. She later went over to the Israelites' side. In the New Testament, this redeemed woman was mentioned in Jesus's genealogy.

● Jesus healed two blind men at Jericho (MATTHEW 20:29–34).

● Zacchaeus was living in Jericho when Jesus came to town. Jesus saw him, invited himself to Zacchaeus's house, and led him to faith (LUKE 19:1–10).

WHERE TO FIND IT IN ISRAEL

Jericho is located about 26 kilometers northeast of Jerusalem. The roads that take a traveler to Jericho are Route 1 east out of Jerusalem and then north on Route 90 near the northwest corner of the Dead Sea.

THINGS TO SEE

◆ *Mount of Temptation:*
Tradition cites this as the place where Satan tempted Jesus with world domination. A cable car can transport visitors up the mountain, which is the location of an ancient monastery built by the Greek Orthodox Church. This current monastery was built in the cliffs of the Mount of Temptation in the late 1800s.

◆ *Tel Jericho:* This archaeological dig has been ongoing for decades, and it explores the ancient city of Jericho. It is a mound that is about sixty feet high and about an acre in size. Visitors can see a stone tower that is said to be several thousand years old.

JERICHO TODAY

Jericho is a Palestinian city of about 20,000 people. It is considered the lowest city in the world at about 850 feet below sea level. Nearly all of the residents of Jericho are of Muslim faith. Christian tourists are free to visit the sites in and around Jericho.

FAVORITE SITE REFLECTION

I still wish I had ridden the **camels**. Now, riding camels in a confined space for no other reason than to be able to report to the people back home that "I rode a camel" is not all that impressive. But saying, "I rode a camel in the oldest city in the world" might raise an eyebrow or two.

Yolanda / Pixabay.com

Imagine viewing a city that is among the oldest cities known to man. And imagine seeing things that have been in use for thousands of years—such as a huge well in the city. Among the things I learned about Jericho from our guide while visiting the city:

● Jericho was considered the world's oldest city by archaeologist Catherine Kenyon.

● There are twenty-three archaeological layers (that's an old city!). The oldest layer is considered pre-stone age.

18

JERUSALEM

*David and all the Israelites marched to **Jerusalem** (that is, Jebus). The Jebusites who lived there said to David, "You will not get in here." Nevertheless, David captured the fortress of Zion—which is the City of David.* **1 CHRONICLES 11:4–5**

WHERE TO FIND IT IN THE BIBLE

Jerusalem is mentioned more than 800 times in the Bible: 1 Kings 11:32, 36;
1 Chronicles 15:1–3; 2 Chronicles 3:1; 20:27–28; Ezra 1:1–3; Psalm 135:21
Jeremiah 4:14; Lamentations 1:17; Mark 11:11; Luke 2:41–51; 23:26–49; A

KEY PASSAGES ABOUT JERUSALEM

66 David and all the Israelites marched to Jerusalem (that is, Jebus). The Jebusites who lived there said to David, "You will not get in here." Nevertheless, David captured the fortress of Zion—which is the City of David. **(1 CHRONICLES 11:4–5)**

66 After David had constructed buildings for himself in the City of David, he prepared a place for the ark of God and pitched a tent for it. **(1 CHRONICLES 15:1)**

66 Then Solomon began to build the temple of the Lord in Jerusalem on Mount Moriah. **(2 CHRONICLES 3:1)**

66 Praise be to the Lord from Zion, to him who dwells in Jerusalem. **(PSALM 135:21)**

66 Jerusalem, wash the evil from your heart and be saved. How long will you harbor wicked thoughts? **(JEREMIAH 4:14)**

66 Many people spread their cloaks on the road, while others spread branches they had cut in the fields. . . . Jesus entered Jerusalem and went into the temple courts. **(MARK 11:8, 11)**

BIBLE STUFF THAT HAPPENED IN JERUSALEM

● It is referred to as the City of David.
● David's army commander Joab attacked the city through the water source and conquered the Jebusites.
● David had the ark of the covenant transferred to Jerusalem.
● David built his palace there.
● Solomon built the first temple there.
● Jerusalem was destroyed by Nebuchadnezzar, and its citizens were sent to Babylon.
● Under Ezra, Zerubbabel, and Nehemiah, the city, the temple, and the walls were

Jerusalem, from the Mount of Olives: Just in front of the golden Dome of the Rock is the Dome of the Tablets. Just behind the dome is the Western Wall. Beyond the wall (blue-gray dome) is the Church of the Holy Sepulchre. At front right is the Garden of Gesthemane. At far left is the City of David and Hezekiah's Tunnel. (Bienchido / Creative Commons)

rebuilt less than one hundred years later.
- The temple was enhanced by King Herod.
- Jesus entered Jerusalem on Palm Sunday as the triumphant king.
- Less than a week later, Jesus was tried, crucified, and resurrected in and just outside Jerusalem.

WHERE TO FIND IT IN ISRAEL

Jerusalem is the largest city in Israel, and it is a city that is sacred to all three of the world's major monotheistic religions: Judaism, Christianity, and Islam. It is located about twenty miles west of the Jordan River and about twenty miles from the Dead Sea's southernmost point. Most tourists fly into Tel Aviv on arrival in Israel, and Jerusalem is about forty miles east of Tel Aviv. Perhaps the cheapest way for a traveler to get from Tel Aviv to Jerusalem is by public bus. It is also possible to take a train from Tel Aviv to the City of David.

THINGS TO SEE

◆ One of the most prominent sites in Jerusalem is the iconic **Dome of the Rock**. This Muslim shrine was built more than 1,300 years ago. The rock over which the building was constructed is, according to tradition, at the location where Abraham went with Isaac to offer him as a sacrifice. While it is possible to visit the Temple Mount itself, non-Muslim visitors cannot enter the Dome of the Rock. This restriction was placed on the Dome in 2000.

Above: **The Western Wall** or Wailing Wall, is the holiest place where Jews are permitted to pray (Terry Bidgood / ODBM).
Right: Part of the **Great Isaiah Scroll**, a copy of which can be seen at the Israel Museum. *Lower right:* The **Church of the Holy Sepulchre** within the Christian Quarter of the walled Old City of Jerusalem (Jorge Láscar / Creative Commons).

◆ The Dome is located on the **Temple Mount**, sometimes referred to as Haram esh-Sharif. This is the traditional site of Solomon's temple and later the second temple.

◆ **The Western Wall:** This is the holiest site for Judaism. It is the wall built during Herod's reign to support the Temple Mount. Jewish men and women come to the Western Wall to pray and to recite Scripture. Some write out their prayers and insert them in cracks between the stones of the wall.

◆ **The Israel Museum:** A facsimile of the Great Isaiah Scroll from the Dead Sea Scrolls is displayed in the Shrine of the Book at the Israel Museum. A portion of

Public domain

the actual scroll can be seen there. Also at the Israel Museum is a 1:50 scale model of Jerusalem during the second temple period.

◆ Locations relating to the passion of Jesus: the **Via Dolorosa**, the **Church of the Holy Sepulchre, Gordon's Calvary,** and so on.

◆ **Old Jerusalem:** Divided into four quarters—the Jewish Quarter, the Christian Quarter, the Armenian Quarter, and the Muslim Quarter. It is fascinating to walk through these areas with their colorful and eclectic shops.

◆ **Jerusalem's walls:** The walls that surround the city today are not from biblical times. Those walls were destroyed by the Romans in AD 70. Subsequent civilizations rebuilt the city walls.

◆ **The Broad Wall:** Archaeologists who uncovered this wall think it was built during the time of King Hezekiah.

◆ **Jerusalem Archaeological Park:** This active archaeological dig is located south of the Temple Mount and the Western Wall. Among the items found is a street from the time of the second temple and King Herod.

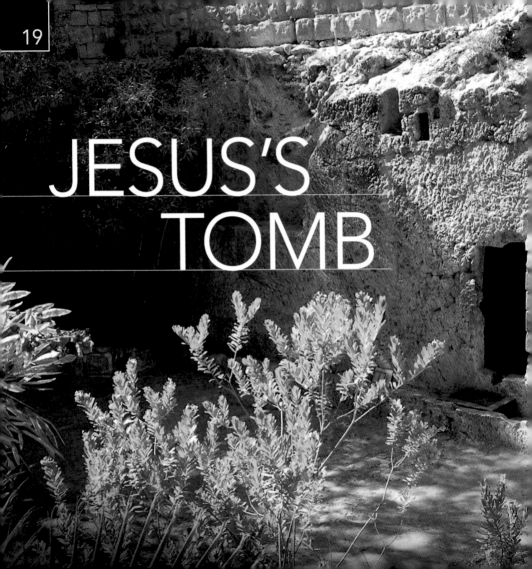

19

JESUS'S
TOMB

*Now there was a man named Joseph, a member of the Council. . . . Going to Pilate, he asked for Jesus' body. Then he took it down, wrapped it in linen cloth and placed it in **a tomb** cut in the rock.* LUKE 23:50, 52–53

WHERE TO FIND IT IN THE BIBLE

Isaiah 53:9; Matthew 27:60; Mark 15:46; Luke 24:1

KEY PASSAGES ABOUT JESUS'S TOMB

❝ He was assigned a grave with the wicked, and with the rich in his death, though he had done no violence, nor was any deceit in his mouth. **(ISAIAH 53:9)**

❝ [Joseph] placed it in his own new tomb that he had cut out of the rock. He rolled a big stone in front of

E GARDEN TOMB, a rock-cut tomb unearthed in 1867, is posed to be Jesus's burial place because of its nearness kull Hill or "Gordon's Calvary." Inside the tomb are partial ains of a burial bench. (Upyernoz / Creative commons)

83

the entrance to the tomb and went away. **(MATTHEW 27:60)**

❝ After the Sabbath, at dawn on the first day of the week, Mary Magdalene and the other Mary went to look at the tomb. **(MATTHEW 28:1)**

❝ So Joseph bought some linen cloth, took down the body, wrapped it in the linen, and placed it in a tomb cut out of rock. Then he rolled a stone against the entrance of the tomb. **(MARK 15:46)**

❝ Very early on the first day of the week, just after sunrise, they were on their way to the tomb. **(MARK 16:2)**

❝ As they entered the tomb, they saw a young man dressed in a white robe sitting on the right side, and they were alarmed. **(MARK 16:5)**

❝ Trembling and bewildered, the women went out and fled from the tomb. They said nothing to anyone, because they were afraid. **(MARK 16:8)**

❝ Joseph took the body, wrapped it in a clean linen cloth, and placed it in his own new tomb that he had cut out of the rock. **(MATTHEW 27:59–60)**

❝ On the first day of the week, very early in the morning, the women took the spices they had prepared and went to the tomb. **(LUKE 24:1)**

❝ When they came back from the tomb, they told all these things to the Eleven and to all the others. **(LUKE 24:9)**

❝ Peter, however, got up and ran to the tomb. Bending over, he saw the strips of linen lying by themselves, and he went

A typical stone tomb located in Mishmar HaEmek, ne Nazareth, Israel. (Alex Soh / Our Daily Bread)

away, wondering to himself what had happened. **(LUKE 24:12)**

❝ Early on the first day of the week, while it was still dark, Mary Magdalene went to the tomb and saw that the stone had been removed from the entrance. **(JOHN 20:1)**

❝ So Peter and the other disciple started for the tomb. **(JOHN 20:3)**

❝ Now Mary stood outside the tomb crying.

As she wept, she bent over to look into the tomb. **(JOHN 20:11)**

❝ In addition, some of our women amazed us. They went to the tomb early this morning. **(LUKE 24:22)**

BIBLE STUFF THAT HAPPENED IN JESUS'S TOMB

All of history centers on this seminal location. From Adam and Eve down through the ages, we see hints and promises and prophecies about a special One who would one day come to be our salvation. That One was murdered on a cross and then put into this borrowed tomb. Who borrows a tomb? Only one who will only need it temporarily. And indeed, Jesus needed it for just three days. On the day after the Sabbath, a sealed tomb is miraculously opened, and Jesus's friends discover that He has left the tomb with His burial linens still inside. And just like that, the promised Messiah broke the bonds of death—not just for himself but for all who would put their faith in Him. What happened here? The greatest miracle ever!

WHERE TO FIND IT IN ISRAEL

As is so often true with the venerated sites in the Holy Land, there's a bit of controversy over the exact location of Jesus's tomb (see Calvary). Since the late nineteenth

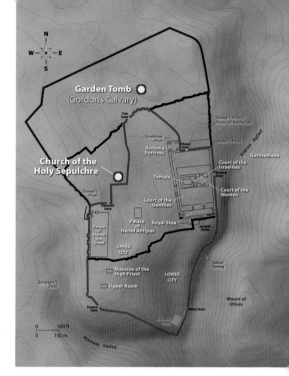

century, there have been two sites that have supporters as the authentic tomb. Therefore, the "Where to Find It" query has two possible answers. The longest-standing claim is held by those who say the Church of the Holy Sepulchre houses Jesus's actual burial site. The more recent claim was made in the 1800s by a British general named Charles Gordon. That tomb site is often referred to as the Garden Tomb. The Church

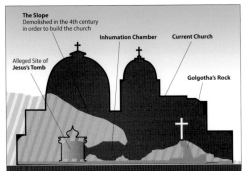

THEN & NOW: *Above:* An illustration of the first century terrain of Golgotha and Christ's Tomb inside the Church of the Holy Sepulchre today (Yupi666 / Creative Commons). *Right:* Inside the church, the tomb of Jesus is said to be located inside this Edicule (shrine), which recently underwent a complete restoration (Terry Bidgood / ODBM).

turned into a display of religious icons and symbols. It is a simple tomb that brings to mind the biblical story of the resurrection in a contemplative way the Church of the Holy Sepulchre can't match.

Most pilgrims also will visit the Church of the Holy Sepulchre. It too has great meaning to many in Christendom. In 2017, a team of archaeologists investigated the

of the Holy Sepulchre is located in the Old City of Jerusalem due east of the Dome of the Rock. The Garden Tomb is outside the Old City walls and on the road that leads out of the Damascus Gate (Nablus Road).

THINGS TO SEE

While no strident claims for authenticity are made by the people who offer the Garden Tomb for visitors, it is still popular for several reasons. One is that the site itself is quiet and beautiful, and Christian worship services are often held on the site. Also, the unadorned setting has not been

tomb by opening its lid. They concluded that the construction materials of the tomb reach back to at least AD 345. When a visitor enters the Church of the Holy Sepulchre, he or she can view several other shrines to Jesus Christ—all of which have an uncertain history as it relates to being authentic: Golgotha (the site of Jesus's crucifixion), the Stone of Unction (where Jesus was pre-pared for burial), and sites relating to Mary Magdalene, St. John, and others. Several religious traditions have assigned sections for their worship items: Greek Orthodox, Catholics, Egyptian Copts, for instance.

JESUS'S TOMB TODAY

What good does it do for us to visit these two sites if neither can categorically claim authenticity? The beauty of having two "competing" burial grounds accentuates the importance of the event that took place at Jesus's tomb. In reality, our inability to say we know for sure which is the true tomb should remind us that we walk by faith, not by sight. Each site can provide worshipful impact. At the Garden, you have time to sit and contemplate that grand morning of Jesus's resurrection, sensing that it may have been a quiet morning such as the one you are enjoying when He burst through death to give life. In the Church, you are reminded that people of a wide range of backgrounds are curious about Jesus and hold Him in high regard. You can pray that they will all recognize the one true reason Jesus came—to give us the free gift of life eternal.

20

JEZREEL VALLEY

JEZREEL VALLEY, here looking south from Nazareth, is a large fertile plain named for the ancient city of Jezreel. The word *Jezreel* comes from the Hebrew, meaning "God sows." (Terry Bidgood / ODBM)

The power of the LORD came on Elijah and, tucking his cloak into his belt, he ran ahead of Ahab all the way to **Jezreel.**

1 KINGS 18:46

WHERE TO FIND IT IN THE BIBLE

Joshua 17:16; Judges 6:33; 1 Samuel 29:11; 1 Kings 18:45; Hosea 1:5

KEY PASSAGES ABOUT THE JEZREEL VALLEY

❝ The people of Joseph replied, "The hill country is not enough for us, and all the Canaanites who live in the plain have chariots fitted with iron, both those in Beth Shan and its settlements and those in the Valley of Jezreel." **(JOSHUA 17:16)**

> Now all the Midianites, Amalekites and other eastern peoples joined forces and crossed over the Jordan and camped in the Valley of Jezreel. **(JUDGES 6:33)**

> In that day I will break Israel's bow in the Valley of Jezreel. **(HOSEA 1:5)**

BIBLE STUFF THAT HAPPENED IN THE JEZREEL VALLEY

To look at the geography of the Jezreel Valley is to get a sense of its importance in biblical history. To the north of the valley are the mountains of Nazareth and Mount Tabor. To the west is Mount Carmel. To the east and the south are Mount Gilboa and the Samarian hills. Each of these areas represented key biblical events. One of the reasons the area was so significant in both biblical and secular history is its location as kind of a crossroads of highways that carried travelers and merchants from far-off locales such as Egypt, Assyria, and Mesopotamia. One of the key highways of ancient times, the Via Maris, intersected the valley.

● The tribe of Manasseh was not able to drive the Canaanites out of Beth Shen (in the Jezreel Valley) because the Canaanites had iron chariots.

● Gideon's conquest of the Midianites took place in the Valley. The men had encamped at Mount Gilboa. On Mount Gilboa, King Saul died.

● The evil king Ahab and his equally dastardly wife Jezebel lived in the Jezreel Valley.

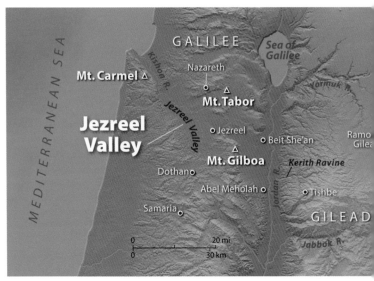

Left: The Jezreel Valley today is known as the breadbasket of Israel. Its main crops include wheat and barley, plus ~~nite~~ beans, chickpeas, cotton, green beans, cowpeas, oranges, sunflowers, corn, squashes, and watermelons. ~~It~~ also has numerous fish ponds that produce various bass, salmon, tilapia, and trout (Tal Oz / Creative Commons). *Right:* ~~A~~t the bottom of Mount Gilboa in the Jezreel Valley is **Ein Harod**, or the "Spring of Harod," which today is part ~~of~~ Ma'ayan Harod National Park (Yair Aronshtam / Creative Commons).

● In this Valley lived the Shunammite woman—the one Elisha assisted by raising her son from the dead.

WHERE TO FIND IT IN ISRAEL

The general area of the Jezreel Valley (about 380 square kilometers) is about an hour and a half northwest of Jerusalem. It is west of Nazareth and just north of the Kishon River. It stretches west to east from Mount Carmel to Beit She'an.

THINGS TO SEE

◆ **Tel Megiddo National Park** (see more information in the section on Megiddo)

◆ From a distance: **Mount Gilboa**, where King Saul fell on his sword and died (**1 SAMUEL 31**).

◆ The valley is heavily farmed because it is flat and fertile for **agriculture**. Cotton and corn are major crops in the area.

◆ From a distance: **Mount Tabor** (see more information in the section on Mount Tabor).

◆ **Ein Harod**, which is the spring of Harod: It was here that Gideon brought his men to thin out the troops by having them drink from the spring. It can be found at the foot of Mount Gilboa.

21

JORDAN
RIVER

THE JORDAN RIVER flows 156 miles north to south through the Sea of Galilee, eventually emptying into the Dead Sea. (Terry Bidgood / ODBM)

*Jesus came from Galilee to the **Jordan** to be baptized by John.* MATTHEW 3:13

WHERE TO FIND IT IN THE BIBLE

Genesis 13:10, 11; 32:10; 50:10, 11; Numbers 13:29; 22:1; 26:3, 63; 31:12; 32:5, 19, 21, 29, 32; 33:48–51; Joshua 1:2; 3:8; 4:18; Job 40:23; Matthew 3:6; Mark 1:5

KEY PASSAGES ABOUT THE JORDAN RIVER

❝ Lot chose for himself the whole plain of the Jordan and set out toward the east. **(GENESIS 13:11)**

❝ The Israelites traveled to the plains of Moab and camped along the Jordan across from Jericho. **(NUMBERS 22:1)**

❝ Moses my servant is dead. Now then, you and all these people, get ready to cross the Jordan River into the land I am about to give them—to the Israelites. **(JOSHUA 1:2)**

❝ The priests who carried the

ark of the covenant of the Lᴏʀᴅ stopped in the middle of the Jordan and stood on dry ground, while all Israel passed by until the whole nation had completed the crossing on dry ground. **(JOSHUA 3:17)**

❝ Gideon and his three hundred men, exhausted yet keeping up the pursuit, came to the Jordan and crossed it. **(JUDGES 8:4)**

BIBLE STUFF THAT HAPPENED AT THE JORDAN RIVER

● One of the most remarkable Bible events that took place at the Jordan River was the crossing of the Israelites into the promised land under the leadership of Joshua. After forty years, it was time for the second generation of wilderness wanderers to enter the land. They had been encamped on the eastern side of the river, stymied by the flooded Jordan. But when the day came for Joshua to lead the people across, an event upriver at the town of Adam stopped the flow of the river. God then dried up the riverbed, and the people lined up behind the ark of the covenant to enter the land **(JOSHUA 3)**.

● Another miracle that relates to the river took place much later, during the time of Elisha. An army commander named Naaman contracted leprosy. Eventually Elisha was asked what he could do about it,

AL-MAGHTAS—meaning "baptism" or "immersion" in Arabic, is an archaeological World Heritage site on the east bank of the Jordan River. This is where Jesus's baptism and the ministry of John the Baptist are believed to have taken place. (Producer / Creative Commons)

and Naaman was told to wash seven times in the Jordan River. The commander felt this was beneath him, but he finally relented, washed in the Jordan, and was healed.

● Above everything else that happened there, though, the baptism of Jesus in the Jordan stands out. It was here that John the Baptist baptized Jesus, and as He came up out of the water, we see the manifestation of the trinity: God the Son, the voice of God the Father, and the appearance of the Holy Spirit descending on Him "in bodily form like a dove" **(LUKE 3:22)**.

WHERE TO FIND IT IN ISRAEL

The Jordan River begins in the far north at the foot of Mount Hermon. Three rivers, the Hasbani, the Dan, and the Banias all converge at the northern tip of the Jordan. It flows south to the Sea of Galilee. That sea then empties into the lower portion of the Jordan, which runs into the Dead Sea.

The most commonly accepted site for the baptism of Jesus is not in Israel; it is in Jordan. A visa is required to cross the border into Jordan to visit Bethany Beyond the Jordan.

THINGS TO SEE

As important as the Jordan River is in biblical history, it's not much to look at today. Irrigation has taken so much of its water away that in some areas the river is nothing more than a small stream.

One of the important things on many tourists' to-do list is to be baptized in the river Jesus was baptized—at the place where he was baptized by John. However, it is impossible to know just where that happened. One candidate is a UNESCO World Heritage site located about seven miles north of the Dead Sea. Archaeological excavations have discovered a number of churches that were said to have been built to mark the site of Jesus's baptism. While this site cannot be verified with certainty,

some contend this was the site. The name of the place is called Bethany Beyond the Jordan. John referred to the place by name in John 1:28. However, the exact site is not known for sure.

The city of Jericho is just west of the Jordan a few miles before it empties into the Dead Sea. This is also the area where Lot chose to settle.

JORDAN RIVER TODAY

The Jordan River is no longer as described in the Bible. In Genesis 13:10 Lot observed that "the whole plain of the Jordan toward Zoar was well watered, like the garden of the LORD." And it is hard to imagine the Jordan being a problem to cross, even at flood stage, as it was for Joshua. Today, it is no more than 50 feet wide at its widest spot.

The Jordan has lost much of its water because of irrigation and other uses of the water. Much of the lush growth that lined the river has also been lost because of the misuse of the river.

22

*When he had finished praying, Jesus left with his disciples and crossed the **Kidron Valley**. On the other side there was a garden, and he and his disciples went into it.*

JOHN 18:1

WHERE TO FIND IT IN THE BIBLE

2 Samuel 15:23; 1 Kings 2:37; 15:13; 2 Kings 23:4, 6, 12; 2 Chronicles 15:16; 29:16; 30:14; Jeremiah 31:40; John 18:1

KEY PASSAGES ABOUT THE KIDRON VALLEY

66 The whole countryside wept aloud as all the people passed by. The king also crossed the Kidron Valley. **(2 SAMUEL 15:23)**

66 The day you leave and cross the Kidron Valley, you can be sure you will die. **(1 KINGS 2:37)**

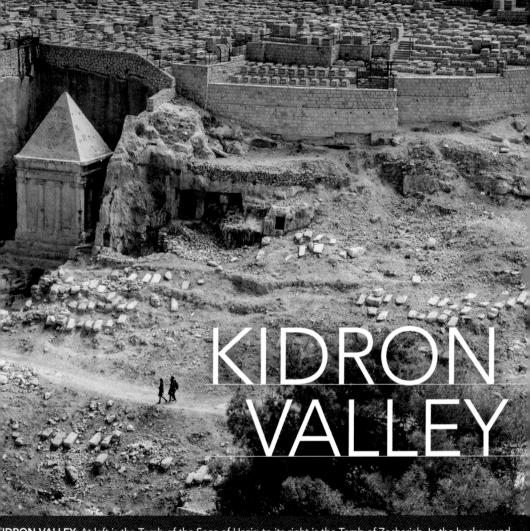

KIDRON VALLEY

KIDRON VALLEY: At left is the Tomb of the Sons of Hazir; to its right is the Tomb of Zechariah. In the background

Above: **Kidron Valley,** as viewed from the Old City of Jerusalem. At lower right is the Millo, a stepped stone structure built by Solomon and rebuilt by Hezekiah (Wilson44691 / Public domain). *Right:* **Absalom's Tomb,** named after King David's rebellious son. For centuries, it was customary for passersby to throw stones at the monument; residents of Jerusalem would bring their unruly children to the site to teach them what became of a rebellious son (Terry Bidgood / ODBM).

❝ The king ordered Hilkiah the high priest, the priests next in rank and the doorkeepers to remove from the temple of the LORD all the articles made for Baal and Asherah and all the starry hosts. He burned them outside Jerusalem in the fields of the Kidron Valley and took the ashes to Bethel. **(2 KINGS 23:4)**

❝ The priests went into the sanctuary of the LORD to purify it. They brought out to the courtyard of the LORD's temple everything unclean that they found in the temple of the LORD. The Levites took it and carried it out to the Kidron Valley. **(2 CHRONICLES 29:16)**

❝ The whole valley where dead bodies and ashes are thrown, and all the terraces out to the Kidron Valley on the east as far as the corner of the Horse Gate, will be holy to the LORD. **(JEREMIAH 31:40)**

BIBLE STUFF THAT HAPPENED IN THE KIDRON VALLEY

Surprisingly, the New Testament mentions the Kidron Valley just one time: John 18:1. So we know for sure that Jesus traveled this valley, which again adds aura to it despite its rather nondescript appearance today. It is the Old Testament that has the most references to this area just outside the walls of Jerusalem.

WHERE TO FIND IT IN ISRAEL

The deep valley called Kidron is east of the walls of the Old City of Jerusalem. It is located between the Temple Mount and the Mount of Olives. **(SEE MAP ON PAGE 85.)**

THINGS TO SEE

◆ As a visitor looks up from the Kidron Valley to the west, he or she will see a hill with a few trees—and then in the distance will be the top of the walls of the *Temple Mount*.

◆ Looking the other direction, one can see the multitude of grave sites that cover the area of the *Mount of Olives*.

◆ In the Valley itself, one can see ancient structures such as large tombs carved out of the side of the Valley. One is called the *Tomb of Pharaoh's Daughter*. Another is named the *Tomb of Zechariah*.

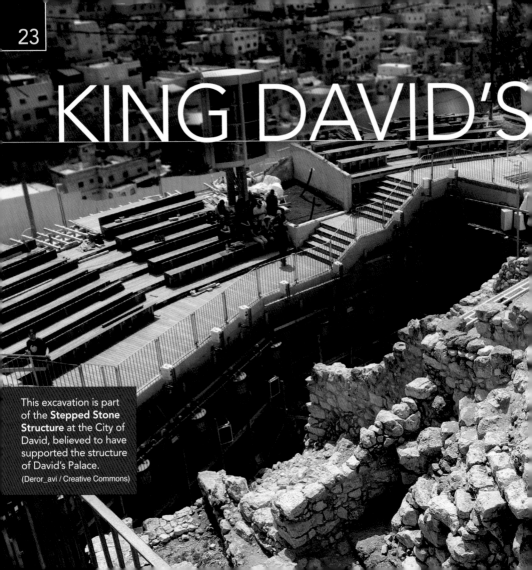

23

KING DAVID'S

This excavation is part of the **Stepped Stone Structure** at the City of David, believed to have supported the structure of David's Palace.
(Deror_avi / Creative Commons)

PALACE

*Now Hiram king of Tyre sent envoys to David, along with cedar logs and carpenters and stonemasons, and they built a **palace for David.***

2 SAMUEL 5:11

WHERE TO FIND IT IN THE BIBLE

2 Samuel 5:11; 1 Chronicles 14:1; 17:1; 28:1; Jeremiah 22:4

KEY PASSAGES ABOUT KING DAVID'S PALACE

❝ One evening David got up from his bed and walked around on the roof of the palace. From the roof he saw a woman bathing. The woman was very beautiful, and David sent someone to find out about her.

(2 SAMUEL 11:2–3)

❝ After David was settled in his palace, he said to Nathan the prophet, "Here I am, living in a house of cedar, while the ark of

the covenant of the LORD is under a tent."
(1 CHRONICLES 17:1)

BIBLE STUFF THAT HAPPENED AT KING DAVID'S PALACE

● It was here that David looked over the lower part of the city and saw Bathsheba on a rooftop.

● David sat in this palace and expressed his sadness that he had a house but God's ark was dwelling in a tent.

WHERE TO FIND IT IN ISRAEL

This archaeological dig is south of the Temple Mount and in the northern tip of what was the City of David in the tenth century BC. It can be found in the same general area as the Gihon Spring and Hezekiah's Tunnel. The area cannot be accessed by car because there is no parking nearby. The best way to get there is by walking through the Dung Gate after leaving the Old City.

THINGS TO SEE

One of Israel's foremost archaeologists, Eilat Mazar, feels confident that she has discovered King David's palace. Located to the south of Jerusalem, this area sparked Mazar's attention because its location fits a passage of Scripture: 2 Samuel 5:17. In that verse, the narrative says David "went down to the stronghold." That would mean that he was going down (south) from his home to a fortress. That was the fortress of Zion mentioned in 2 Samuel 5:7. Mazar feels that the large stone structure she found and the massive step-stone structure are left over from David's day.

Among the artifacts discovered at this

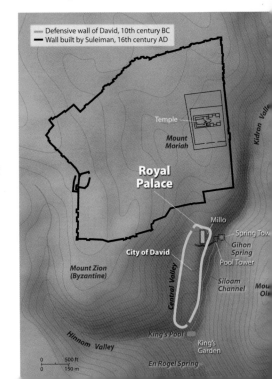

bove: Another angle of the Stepped Stone
ructure (Ian W. Scott / Creative Commons). *Right: "The*
arge Stone Structure" is the name given to a set
f remains interpreted by Israeli archaeologist
lat Mazar, and is near the Stepped Stone
ructure. Mazar believes it may be the remains of
ng David's palace as recorded in 1 and 2 Samuel
eror avi / Creative Commons).

location is a bulla, a small seal made
from a clay impression. The discovered
bullae had this name on it: Yehuchal ben
Shelemiyahu. His name is mentioned in
the Bible in Jeremiah 38:1. But that's not
all. Another bullae was discovered close
by a couple of years later. On this one
was the name of Gedaliah, son of Pashur.
That name is found in the same verse as
Shelemiyahu. Astounding. They are on
display at the Israel Museum.

The area of the palace that has been
excavated is covered, and visitors can see
some of the stone structure by descending
stairs. According to Mazar, there are
two structures to see there: the ruins of
the palace and the step structure that
she surmises held up the foundations of
the palace.

24

KORAZIM (CHORAZIN)

*Woe to you, **Chorazin!** Woe to you, Bethsaida! For if the miracles that were performed in you had been performed in Tyre and Sidon, they would have repented long ago in sackcloth and ashes.*

MATTHEW 11:21

At the center of Korazim's ruins is a large, impressive synagogue built with black basalt stones and decorated with Jewish motifs. It was built in the late third century, destroyed in the fourth century, and rebuilt in the sixth century.

(Jim Black / Pixabay.com)

WHERE TO FIND IT IN THE BIBLE

Matthew 11:20–22;
Luke 10:13–14

KEY PASSAGE ABOUT KORAZIM
(modern name for Chorazin)

❝ Woe to you Chorazin! Woe to you, Bethsaida! For if the miracles that were performed in you had been performed in Tyre and Sidon, they would have repented long ago, in sackcloth and ashes. **(MATTHEW 11:21)**

BIBLE STUFF THAT HAPPENED AT KORAZIM

● We know for sure that miracles occurred in Korazim, and we can know that Jesus participated in them. In His warnings in Matthew and Luke, Jesus talked about "the miracles that were performed in you." And in Matthew 11:20, the writer said, "Jesus began to denounce the towns in which most of his miracles had been performed." And in the next verse Korazim is mentioned.

● We can also surmise that Jesus spent time in Korazim because nearby Capernaum was His base for some time. Also, there was a third-century synagogue at Korazim. Capernaum also had a later synagogue (later than first century), but we know that Jesus spoke in that city from an earlier synagogue. Perhaps He did the same in Korazim.

Near right: Basalt stone ruins at Korazim National Park (Terry Bidgood / ODBM). *Above:* This stone chair, inscribed in Aramaic, was known as the "Seat of Moses" (Pikiwikisrael / Creative Commons). *Right top:* One of several olive millstones at Korazim (Effib / Creative Commons). *Lower right:* The decorated architecture of the synagogue includes images of Medusa, indicating that other religions had crept into Jewish worship (Hoshvilim / Creative Commons).

WHERE TO FIND IT IN ISRAEL

Northwest of the Sea of Galilee and near the cities of Capernaum and Bethsaida lies Korazim. It is located just over two miles north of Capernaum. The area of Korazim can be reached by car but not by public transportation. **(SEE MAP ON PAGE 22)**

THINGS TO SEE

On the site of this ancient, cursed city is Korazim National Park. What visitors can see are ruins of the town from around the fourth or fifth century AD. The main structure is **the remains of a synagogue**. One impressive finding in the remains of this building was something called the **"Seat of Moses."** Jesus referred to the concept of this seat in Matthew 23:2. It was, perhaps, a special seat for dignitaries to use during Torah readings.

25

The steps and Corinthian columns at right are part of "Temple A" and were built in the second century AD. Originally dedicated to Apollo, Artemis, and Aphrodite, the building transformed into a church archive in the

*I want you to know how hard I am contending for you and for those at **Laodicea**, and for all who have not met me personally.*

COLOSSIANS 2:1

LAODICEA

rth century. It was greatly damaged by two earthquakes in the fifth and seventh centuries. In the background to left are the columns of the North (or Sacred) Agora. (Carole Raddato / Creative Commons)

WHERE TO FIND IT IN THE BIBLE

Colossians 2:1; 4:13, 15–16; Revelation 1:11; 3:14

KEY PASSAGES ABOUT LAODICEA

❝ I vouch for [Epaphras] that he is working hard for you and for those at Laodicea and Hierapolis. **(COLOSSIANS 4:13)**

> ❝ To the angel of the church in Laodicea write: These are the words of the Amen, the faithful and true witness, the ruler of God's creation. **(REVELATION 3:14)**

BIBLE STUFF THAT HAPPENED AT LAODICEA

● Two Bible writers referred to Laodicea. Paul mentioned it twice in Colossians, once to let the people know that he recognized the struggles they were enduring (just as he had done to Philippi in Philippians 1:30). The second time Paul mentioned the city, it was in regard to the work of Epaphras, who had influenced the people in Laodicea, in Hierapolis, and in Colossae **(COLOSSIANS 1:7)**.

● John most famously wrote about Laodicea in the book of Revelation. In chapter 3 the apostle told the people of Laodicea's church that they were guilty of being neither hot or cold in their dedication to "deeds" **(v. 15)**. They were lukewarm and were to change their ways.

WHERE TO FIND IT IN TURKEY

About three and a half hours inland from the Aegean Sea is the city of Denizli, home to more than half a million people. Laodicea is located just a few miles north of Denizli, and it can be reached by minibus or by car quite readily. A high-speed train also can take tourists from Ankara to Denizli.

THINGS TO SEE

◆ Excavations of the ruins of Laodicea began in earnest in this century, and visitors can now see the basic layout to the city in biblical times. Items such as the city's *agora* and its *column-lined seats* indicate that the city was quite wealthy.

◆ A *church* was discovered in 2010, but experts do not think it was the actual church building of the first century—but one from a couple of centuries later. Also, some **temples** have been unearthed in the excavations.

◆ A large number of **other buildings, structures, and places of entertain-ment** have been discovered in Laodicea. Included in the finds have been several other churches in the city.

◆ The city of Laodicea that we know from Bible days no longer exists. It was destroyed by a series of earthquakes through the centuries. However, archaeologists have painstakingly restored much of the main areas of Laodicea over their years of study.

Covered interior of a fourth century Laodicean Christian church. On the center floor are the remains of the **ambo**—a raised platform for reading and preaching—akin to a bimah in Jewish synagogues. (Blcksprt / Creative Commons)

26

Magdala—an entire first century Galileean town—was discovered in 2009. One of the first structures found was this **synagogue,** where it is certain that Jesus taught. Here they found the **Magdala Stone** *(left center),* called the most significant archaeological find of the past fifty years. (Carole Raddato / Creative Commons)

Mary Magdalene went to the disciples with the news: "I have seen the Lord!"

JOHN 20:18

MAGDALA

WHERE TO FIND IT IN THE BIBLE

Matthew 27:56; Mark 16:9; Luke 8:2; John 19:25; 20:18

KEY PASSAGES ABOUT MAGDALA

❝ Some women who had been cured of evil spirits and diseases: Mary (called Magdalene). **(LUKE 8:2)**

❝ Near the cross of Jesus stood his mother, his mother's

sister, Mary the wife of Clopas, and Mary Magdalene. **(JOHN 19:25)**

❝ When Jesus rose early on the first day of the week, he appeared first to Mary Magdalene, out of whom he had driven seven demons. **(MARK 16:9)**

BIBLE STUFF THAT HAPPENED AT MAGDALA

No direct mention of the Galilean town of Magdala is made in Scripture. However, the ancient town near Capernaum is considered by experts to be the home of one of the New Testament's most faithful women: Mary Magdalene. It is rather evident from findings of archaeologists and from Jesus's travels that He most assuredly visited Magdala.

Below: Magdala's numerous excavations and visitor center as seen from above on the northwest shore of the Sea of Galilee (AVRAMGR / Creative Commons). *Right:* One of two discovered **miqva'ot**—Jewish ritual baths used for immersion to achieve purity. These were fed by groundwater flowing through the unsealed rock walls (Bukvoed / Creative Commons).

have been unearthed by archaeologists. According to the Magdala website, a first-century coin was found inside the synagogue. It was minted in AD 29, which corresponds with the years of Jesus's ministry. It is very possible that Jesus taught in that synagogue.

◆ In 2009, a remarkable archaeological relic was uncovered at that site. It is called **the Magdala Stone**, a stone box carved on its sides with depictions of a temple and a menorah. It is thought that the carvings represent the Second Temple in Jerusalem. The original, which was on display briefly at the Vatican, is in safekeeping, but a replica can be seen at Magdala.

◆ A vibrant new **visitor center** has been built at Magdala to accommodate the growing numbers or people interested in the newly discovered archaeological finds at this location, including the synagogue. You can learn more at **magdala.org**.

WHERE TO FIND IT IN ISRAEL

Magdala is located near the current town of Migdal, which is on the shore of the Sea of Galilee. The excavation of Magdala is on the western coast of the Sea. It is about eight miles west and south of Capernaum. It takes about two hours to get from Jerusalem to Magdala by car. (SEE MAP ON PAGE 34.)

THINGS TO SEE

The traditional hometown of Mary Magdalene was a substantial urban center in the days of Jesus on earth. It was destroyed by Roman soldiers about thirty years after Jesus's crucifixion, resurrection, and ascension.

◆ The ruins of a **first-century synagogue**

27

MEGIDDO

*Here is the account of the forced labor King Solomon conscripted to build the LORD's temple, his own palace, the terraces, the wall of Jerusalem, and Hazor, **Megiddo** and Gezer.* **1 KINGS 9:15**

The strategic city of **Megiddo** has been built, leveled, and rebuilt over twenty times (twenty-five strata). Archaeologists have uncovered ruins that tell of the many cultures and people living there, including the nation of Israel. The round flat structure at right was an open-air sacrificial altar built around 2700 BC, in the area of the former great temple.
(Terry Bidgood / ODBM)

WHERE TO FIND IT IN THE BIBLE

Joshua 12:21; 17:11; Judges 1:27; 5:19; 1 Kings 4:12; 9:15; 2 Kings 9:27; 23:29–30; 1 Chronicles 7:29; 2 Chronicles 35:22; Zechariah 12:11

KEY PASSAGES ABOUT MEGIDDO

❝ Manasseh did not drive out the people of Beth Shan or Taanach or Dor or Ibleam or Megiddo and their surrounding settlements, for the Canaanites were determined to live in that land. **(JUDGES 1:27)**

66 When Ahaziah king of Judah saw what had happened, he fled up the road to Beth Haggan. Jehu chased him, shouting, "Kill him too!" They wounded him in his chariot on the way up to Gur near Ibleam, but he escaped to Megiddo and died there. **(2 KINGS 9:27)**

66 While Josiah was king, Pharaoh Necho king of Egypt went up to the Euphrates River to help the king of Assyria. King Josiah marched out to meet him in battle, but Necho faced him and killed him at Megiddo. **(2 KINGS 23:29)**

BIBLE STUFF THAT HAPPENED AT MEGIDDO

● The ancient city of Megiddo was one of the cities defeated by the Hebrews after they entered the Promised Land and were charged with conquering the people who lived there **(JOSHUA 12:21)**.

● The city of Megiddo was built up under the auspices of King Solomon **(1 KINGS 9:15)**. It became a key city in the region, and it had sophisticated water systems and palaces.

● King Ahaziah of Judah died at Megiddo after being chased by Jehu, who had been given the task of destroying the household of Ahab (of which Ahaziah was a part). Ahaziah was wounded while traveling in his chariot and escaped to Megiddo, where he died **(2 KINGS 9:27)**.

● King Josiah was helping Assyria fight against Egypt. He faced off against Pharaoh Necho, who killed Josiah at Megiddo **(2 KINGS 23:29)**.

● The book of Revelation pinpoints Megiddo (Armageddon) as the site of the

Left: This large circular pit was a grain silo during King Jeroboam II's reign in the eighth century BC (Terry Bidgood / ODBM). *Above:* Megiddo's underground waterworks, built in the tenth century BC. It has 183 stairs leading down 36M, and a 70M tunnel leading to the spring under the bedrock, which supplied water to the city and allowed it to survive long military sieges (Terry Bidgood / ODBM).

last great battle before Jesus's second coming (**REVELATION 16:13–16**).

WHERE TO FIND IT IN ISRAEL

Megiddo is located about twenty miles southeast of the city of Haifa. It is located on Route 66, which can be taken from Haifa to the site. From Jerusalem, take Route 1 north to Route 6. From 6, take 65 to Tel Megiddo Street in Megiddo. (**SEE MAP ON PAGE 38.**)

THINGS TO SEE AT MEGIDDO

Megiddo is so old that there are twenty-six layers at Tel Megiddo, each representing a different civilization that lived there.[9] Therefore, Megiddo is a major archaeological dig. The area is called Megiddo National Park, and it has been designated a World Heritage Site by UNESCO. The area has been the object of several archaeological excavations.

◆ A *high place* from the time of the Canaanites.

◆ A large *grain pit* that was used to ensure a food supply for the Israelites if the city were under siege. It is thought to have been in use during the reign of King Jeroboam in the eighth century BC.

◆ *Solomon-era city gates* and *stables*.

◆ A huge *water system* that was an amazing engineering feat. It included a vertical shaft that is 180 feet deep and a tunnel that is longer than a football field.

◆ A thousands-of-years-old *temple*.

FAVORITE SITE REFLECTION

The mystique of this site has its own value. Just arriving at this site automatically calls to mind not only the significance of its past but the spellbinding importance of its future. At most locations in Israel, your mind tries to recall past events and people you've read about in Scripture. Megiddo, though, puts the future into focus. On this spot at some future time, the end of the earth as we know it will occur. In an event that the mind can't even imagine, Jesus Christ will return in the air to settle the last great battle of all time.

28

MOUNT

Now when Jesus saw the crowds, he went up on a mountainside and sat down. His disciples came to him, and he began to teach them. **MATTHEW 5:1–2**

OF BEATITUDES

Looking south from the Mount and the grounds of the Church of the Beatitudes offers a great view of the Sea of Galilee. On the far right shore is Tiberias. (Olevy / Creative Commons)

WHERE TO FIND IT IN THE BIBLE

Matthew 5:1–8:1

KEY PASSAGES ABOUT THE MOUNT OF BEATITUDES

❝ Now when Jesus saw the crowds, he went up on a mountainside and sat down. His disciples came to him, and he began to teach them. **(MATTHEW 5:1–2)**

❝ When Jesus came down from the mountainside, large crowds followed him. **(MATTHEW 8:1)**

BIBLE STUFF THAT HAPPENED ON THE MOUNT

Large crowds had been following Jesus, and He had gone up to a mountainside in the region of the Sea of Galilee. He sat down, the disciples joined Him, and He began to teach.

To visit this site and see the natural amphitheater-like sloping hill and to hear that the sound of a voice can carry well on the hill

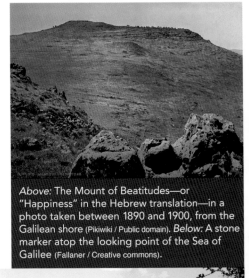

Above: The Mount of Beatitudes—or "Happiness" in the Hebrew translation—in a photo taken between 1890 and 1900, from the Galilean shore (Pikiwiki / Public domain). *Below:* A stone marker atop the looking point of the Sea of Galilee (Fallaner / Creative commons).

THE MOUNT OF BEATITUDES TODAY

The **Church of the Beatitudes** is a beautiful, octagonal worship place overlooking the traditional Mount of Beatitudes. According to the *Archaeology Study Bible*, there are two possible reasons for the eight-sided nature of the building. One, it could have been built that way to "commemorate the eight beatitudes," or it could have been a characteristic church design of Byzantine architects.[10]

Heather Truett / Pixabay.com

Visitors often hear or themselves recite the Beatitudes while standing on what is believed by most to be the actual site of Jesus's sermon.

leads one to imagine that this could be the place where Jesus addressed the multitude.

WHERE TO FIND IT IN ISRAEL

Most experts think the location for Jesus's Sermon on the Mount was between the towns Tabgha and Capernaum, overlooking the Sea of Galilee. Motoring from Tiberias north to these towns is a trip of about ten miles. **(SEE MAP ON PAGE 34.)**

THINGS TO SEE

◆ In the vicinity of the hill is a chapel built in the 1930s by the Franciscan Sisters. It is called the Church of the Beatitudes.
◆ The view from the mount is spectacular, giving the visitor a panoramic look at the sea on which Jesus traveled so frequently. It is possible to see Capernaum, which is just a couple of miles away.

29

MOUNT CARMEL

The southwest face of **Mount Carmel** during the sunset. Mount Carmel is part of a coastal mountain range in northern Israel that stretches from the Mediterranean Sea toward the southeast and overlooks the fertile Jezreel Valley. One purported place where the famed offering of Elijah took place is on the mountain at a monastery,

*[Elijah replied,] "Now summon the people from all over Israel to meet me on **Mount Carmel**. And bring the four hundred and fifty prophets of Baal and the four hundred prophets of Asherah, who eat at Jezebel's table."* **1 KINGS 18:19**

built in 1868, called El-Muhraqa ("the burning"), possibly referring to the consuming fire that rained down on Elijah's sacrifice. The site is also favored because it has a spring, from which water could have been drawn to drench the offering. (Chadner / Public domain)

WHERE TO FIND IT IN THE BIBLE

1 Kings 18:19, 20; 2 Kings 2:25; 4:25; Song of Songs 7:5; Jeremiah 46:18

KEY PASSAGES ABOUT MOUNT CARMEL

❝ Ahab sent word throughout all Israel and assembled the prophets on Mount Carmel. **(1 KINGS 18:20)**

❝ So she set out and came to the man of God at Mount Carmel. When he saw her in the distance, the man of

God said to his servant Gehazi, "Look! There's the Shunammite!" **(2 KINGS 4:25)**

BIBLE STUFF THAT HAPPENED AT MOUNT CARMEL

● Here's a Bible story with both drama and humor! Of course, the drama of the most famous incident at Mount Carmel was Elijah's amazing challenge to the prophets of Baal. Here was a prophet of God calling out the men who claimed that Baal was real. Prove it, Elijah said. In essence, he was saying, "Have your god set fire to the sacrifice, and we'll say he's the real God." The humor of the incident is Elijah's trash-talking of the prophets. Speaking of the inactivity of their gods, Elijah suggested that they were asleep—or perhaps "sitting on the toilet" **(1 KINGS 18:27 TLB)**. Of course, Elijah was the only one laughing. Then he proceeded to nearly drown the sacrifice with water, call on God, and stand back as God zapped the sacrifice and set it all on fire.

● Elijah's successor, Elisha, returned to Mount Carmel after a strange incident in which some young people mocked him by calling him "You baldhead" and were then dispatched by a couple of bears **(2 KINGS 2:23–25 NASB)**.

WHERE TO FIND IT IN ISRAEL

Mount Carmel is located near the Mediterranean Coast of Israel, near the city of Haifa. If you look at a map of Israel, you'll see Mount Carmel southeast of the little peninsula-type landform far north of Caesarea and almost directly west of the Sea of Galilee. It is about an hour and a half by car from Jerusalem. Take Route 1 westbound from Jerusalem and turn north on Route 6 to get to Mount Carmel.

MOUNT CARMEL TODAY

To access the traditional site of Elijah's thrilling victory over the false gods of Baal, visitors climb the mountain to the Stella Maris Carmelite Monastery. This overlooks the sloping location of the story told in 1 Kings 18. Also, a statue of Elijah stands sentry over the location.

FAVORITE SITE REFLECTION

We've all been to places that offer spectacular views because they overlook majestic settings. Viewing Chicago from the Willis Tower. Standing in the tower at Clingman's Dome in the Great Smoky Mountains. Climbing to the top of Sleeping Bear Sand Dunes in northern Michigan and gazing over the matchless beauty of Glen Lake. Taking the steps up to a higher level of the Eiffel Tower and getting a bird's-eye view of the City of Lights. That is what it is like to be on Mount Carmel and gain a perspective of the Jezreel Valley and all of the sights on the panorama of the horizon. Our guide told us what we were seeing: Look below and into the near distance to see the valley through which Elijah ran to escape Jezebel. Look in this direction, and you can see Mount Tabor. Look in another direction to see Megiddo, the valley of the final battle. So, in addition to being able to imagine Elijah's battle with the pagan gods, Mount Carmel gives a sweeping view of many other key places in biblical geography. The view is magnificent!

Terry Bidgood / ODBM

30

Mount Ebal (right) from Mount Gerizim. Between the two mounts lies the nearly Two-thousand-year-old city of Nablus. Founded by Roman Emperor Vespasian (AD 72), the city has been under the rule of many empires. (Terry Bidgood / ODBM)

Then Joshua built on **Mount Ebal** *an altar to the LORD, the God of Israel.*

JOSHUA 8:30

MOUNT EBAL

WHERE TO FIND IT IN THE BIBLE

Deuteronomy 11:29; 27:1, 4, 13; Joshua 8:30, 33

KEY PASSAGE ABOUT MOUNT EBAL

66 All the Israelites, with their elders, officials and judges, were standing on both sides of the ark of the covenant of the Lord, facing the Levitical priests who carried it.

Above: The view from Mount Ebal across the vale of Shechem to Mount Gerizim. (Someone35; / Creative Commons). *Above right:* The archaeological site believed to be the stones of Joshua's Altar on Mount Ebal, looking west (Daniel Ventura / Creative Commons).

Both the foreigners living among them and the native-born were there. Half of the people stood in front of Mount Gerizim and half of them in front of Mount Ebal, as Moses the servant of the LORD had formerly commanded when he gave instructions to bless the people of Israel. **(JOSHUA 8:33)**

❝ When you have crossed the Jordan, set up these stones on Mount Ebal, as I command you today, and coat them with plaster. **(DEUTERONOMY 27:4)**

BIBLE STUFF THAT HAPPENED AT MOUNT EBAL

We might call it the Sermon on the Two Mounts. The city of Shechem sat at the base of two mountains: Mount Ebal to the east and Mount Gerizim to the west.

WHERE TO FIND IT IN ISRAEL

Mount Ebal is about an hour and a half from Jerusalem by road. Using Route 50, a traveler would go to Route 1 until it becomes Route 6. After forty minutes, take Route 444, then Route 55 and on to Route 60. It is located about midway to the west of the

Jordan—about halfway between the Sea of Galilee and the Dead Sea. And it lies about halfway (east and west) between the Jordan River and the Mediterranean Sea.

The area cannot be accessed freely by all, so any visitor must be aware of restrictions that relate to the home country and even the religion of visitors.

THINGS TO SEE

◆ *Mount Ebal* rises to a peak of just over three thousand feet, and it occupies under seven square miles in area. The mountain is made of limestone, and it is characterized by a number of large caverns.

◆ *Joshua's Altar:* A grand archaeological discovery is a rock mound that some scholars say is an altar built by Joshua. Visitation to the site is limited by the political situation in Israel, so it is possible that a visitor won't be allowed to gain access to it.

*After six days Jesus took Peter, James and John with him and led them up a **high mountain**, where they were all alone. There he was transfigured before them.* MARK 9:2

31

MOUNT HERMON

WHERE TO FIND IT IN THE BIBLE

Deuteronomy 3:8; 4:48; Joshua 11:17; 12:1, 5; 13:5, 11; Judges 3:3; 1 Chronicles 5:23; Psalm 42:6; 133:3; Song of Songs 4:8; Mark 9:2, Luke 9:28–30

KEY PASSAGES ABOUT MOUNT HERMON

❝ So Joshua took this entire land: the hill country, all the Negev, the

Mount Hermon is part of the Anti-Lebanon mountain range. Its highest point is 9,230 feet above sea level and is on the border between Syria and Lebanon; it is now under Syrian control. Part of the southern slopes fall within the Golan Heights, an area under Israeli control since the 1967 war. (Konstantnin / Shutterstock.com)

whole region of Goshen, the western foothills, the Arabah and the mountains of Israel with their foothills, from Mount Halak, which rises toward Seir, to Baal Gad in the Valley of Lebanon below Mount Hermon. **(JOSHUA 11:16–17)**

❝ It is as if the dew of Hermon were falling on Mount Zion. **(PSALM 133:3)**

❝ [Jesus] took Peter, John and James with him and went onto a mountain to pray. As he was praying, the appearance of his face changed, and his clothes became as bright as a flash of lightning. Two men, Moses and Elijah, appeared. **(LUKE 9:28–30)**

BIBLE STUFF THAT HAPPENED AT MOUNT HERMON

● As were Dan and Beersheba, Mount Hermon was often used as a geographic marker in the Bible. This was true in Deuteronomy 3:8: "territory east of the Jordan, from the Arnon Gorge as far as Mount Hermon." The Arnon Gorge is a bit past north of halfway down the Dead Sea to the east, and Mount Hermon is far north where the Jordan River begins. Deuteronomy 4:48 and Joshua 11:17 also use Mount Hermon as a geographic marker.
● In Joshua 12 we discover that a king who ruled over Mount Hermon at one time was Og, king of Bashan. Several

Left: Waterfall on the El-Al river (Public domain). *Above:* The Banias Waterfall in the Golan Heights (NahumDam / Public domain). *Right:* Mount Hermon Ski Resort (Iman Shahin / Pikiwiki Israel).

the spot where Peter confessed Jesus as Messiah and probably near the site of the transfiguration.

WHERE TO FIND IT IN ISRAEL

Located at the far north of Israel, Mount Hermon is about 120 miles from Jerusalem. It is a nearly four-hour drive from the City of David to the mountain. Parts of Mount Hermon are in Syria and other surrounding countries. (SEE MAP ON PAGE 38.)

THINGS TO SEE

◆ *Snow:* Mount Hermon is the only place in Israel where you can see snow. There is a ski resort on Mount Hermon.

◆ *Banias:* Also, at the foot of Mount Hermon is Banias, mentioned elsewhere in this book as a pagan place where Jesus taught His disciples about what was going to happen next in their adventure together. It is also known as Caesarea Philippi.

other references tell who lived in the area of Mount Hermon.

● The most significant event relating to Mount Hermon was when Jesus took His disciples to Caesarea Philippi, which is at the base of Mount Hermon. This was

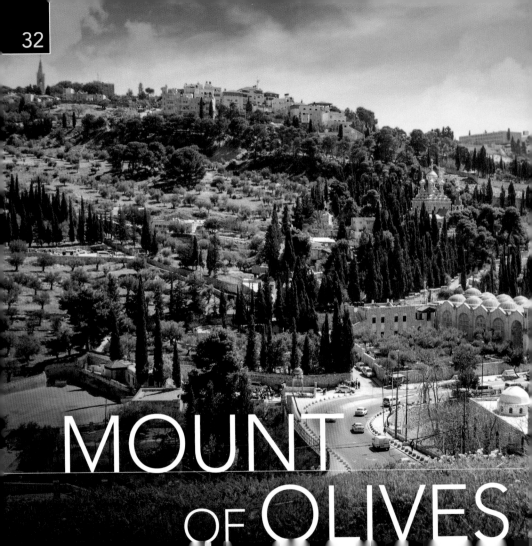

32

MOUNT
OF OLIVES

Terry Bidgood / ODBM

*When they had sung a hymn, they went out to the **Mount of Olives.***

MATTHEW 26:30

WHERE TO FIND IT IN THE BIBLE

2 Samuel 15:30; Zechariah 14:4; Matthew 21:1; 24:3; 26:30; Mark 11:1; 13:3; 14:26; Luke 19:29, 37; 21:37; 22:39; John 8:1; Acts 1:12

KEY PASSAGES ABOUT THE MOUNT OF OLIVES

❝ On that day his feet will stand on the Mount of Olives, east of Jerusalem, and the Mount of Olives will be split in two from east to west, forming a great valley, with half of the mountain moving north and half moving south. **(ZECHARIAH 14:4)**

❝ As Jesus was sitting on the Mount of Olives, the disciples came to him privately. "Tell us," they said, "when will this happen, and what will be the sign of your coming and of the end of the age?" **(MATTHEW 24:3)**

137

BIBLE STUFF THAT HAPPENED ON THE MOUNT OF OLIVES

● Let's start with something that will happen someday in the future—as mentioned in the Old Testament. In Zechariah 14:4, the prophet prophesies about a time when Jesus will return to the Mount of Olives. In Acts 1, after Jesus ascended to heaven from the Mount of Olives, two angels said that Jesus "will come back in the same way you have seen him go into heaven" (v. 11). This is another mention of the upcoming event mentioned in Zechariah.

● King David ascended the Mount of Olives outside Jerusalem—just as many did hundreds of years later in Jesus's day. The text of 2 Samuel 15 doesn't say specifically why David was weeping and had his head covered, but it was perhaps because of the rebellion of his son Absalom.

● In the New Testament, Jesus is often on the Mount of Olives. In Matthew 24 He was sitting on the Mount when His disciples asked about the end of the age. In Matthew 26, He and His disciples "went out to the Mount of Olives" (v. 30) after the disciples had partaken of the Lord's Supper and had sung a hymn.

● It was while at the Mount of Olives that Jesus sent two disciples to get a donkey for His triumphal entry. And it was while approaching Jerusalem from the Mount of Olives that Jesus wept over the city (LUKE 19:41). He would have climbed the eastern slope of the Mount of Olives and down the western slope, across the Kidron Valley and into Jerusalem.

"In that day His feet will stand on the Mount of Olives...."
(ZECHARIAH 14:4 NASB)

Left: Sunset over Jerusalem as seen from the Mount of Olives (Krystian / Pixabay.com).
Above: The Jewish Cemetery on the mount (R-Janke / Pixabay.com).
Right: The Dome of the Ascension (David Castor / Creative Commons).

WHERE TO FIND IT IN ISRAEL

The Mount of Olives is a two-mile-long ridge that stands to the east of Jerusalem. The elevation of the Mount of Olives is higher than that of Jerusalem by about three hundred feet.[11] The town of Bethany, so familiar to Jesus, rests on the eastern slope of the Mount of Olives. The Temple Mount is directly west of the Mount of Olives, and between the two is Gethsemane. **(SEE MAPS ON PAGES 85 AND 102.)**

THINGS TO SEE

◆ All three major monotheistic world religions have **cemeteries** in the area of the Mount of Olives. The selection of this location for the final resting place of Jews, Muslims, and Christians probably relates to the Zechariah 14:4 prophecy of Jesus's return.

◆ *Jerusalem:* From the Mount of Olives, you get the iconic view of the Old City of Jerusalem with the Dome of the Rock dominating the landscape.

◆ If you like places of worship, the Mount of Olives has several historic churches, synagogues, and mosques. While shrines are not certain indicators of biblical events, you could visit the **Dome of the Ascension** (the traditional site of Jesus's ascension) on the top of the Mount. A walk down the hill and to the southwest will take you to the **Tomb of the Virgin Mary**—the place where many say Jesus's mother Mary was buried.

◆ In that same area is the **garden of Gethsemane**, a definite must-see. Although we know the general location of the garden on the western slope of the Mount of Olives, archaeologists cannot pinpoint the exact location. There are olive trees in the area, but none are the original trees from Jesus's day. While olive trees can grow to be two thousand years old (a tree on the island of Crete is said to be at least that old[12]), but Romans cut down all of the trees of Jerusalem in AD 70.[13]

33

MOUNT TABOR

Mount Tabor is at the eastern end of the Jezreel Valley, eleven miles west of the Sea of Galilee. In the Old Testament, it is the site of the battle between the Israelite army, led by Barak, and the Canaanite army, commanded by Sisera. From the New Testament, Mount Tabor is believed by some to be the site of the transfiguration of Jesus. (Terry Bidgood / ODBM)

Then Deborah said to Barak, "Go! This is the day the LORD has given Sisera into your hands. Has not the LORD gone ahead of you?" So Barak went down Mount Tabor, with ten thousand men following him. **JUDGES 4:14**

WHERE TO FIND IT IN THE BIBLE

Joshua 19:12, 22, 34; Judges 4:6, 12, 14; 8:18; 1 Samuel 10:3; 1 Chronicles 6:77; Psalm 89:12; Jeremiah 46:18; Hosea 5:1

KEY PASSAGES ABOUT MOUNT TABOR

❝ She sent for Barak son of Abinoam from Kedesh in Naphtali and said to him, "The LORD, the God of Israel, commands you: 'Go, take with you ten thousand men of Naphtali and Zebulun and lead them up to Mount Tabor.'" **(JUDGES 4:6)**

❝ Then Deborah said to Barak, "Go! This is the day the LORD has given Sisera into your hands. Has not the LORD gone ahead of you?" So Barak went down Mount Tabor, with ten thousand men following him. **(JUDGES 4:14)**

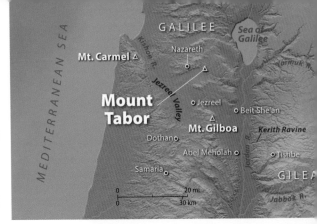

BIBLE STUFF THAT HAPPENED AT MOUNT TABOR

The most famous Bible incident at Mount Tabor was the story of the teamwork of Barak and Deborah to fight off the Canaanites.

WHERE TO FIND IT IN ISRAEL

With an elevation at its peak of 1,886 feet, Mount Tabor is not hard to find. It is located at the eastern end of the Jezreel Valley—just over ten miles west of the Sea of Galilee. It offers a panoramic view of the Jezreel Valley, and one can even see Mount Hermon to the north from its top. Visitors can access its peak either by car or by hiking. If you don't have a car, a taxi service is available.

Above, right: The Basilica of the Transfiguration (Franciscan) was built on the ruins of a Byzantine church (sixth century) and a later church of the Crusader Kingdom period (Bahnfrend / Creative Commons). *Right:* Overlooking the village of Daburiyya and the Jezreel Valley from Mount Tabor (Tiamat / Creative Commons).

THINGS TO SEE

◆ Just looking at Mount Tabor helps a visitor imagine why Jeremiah uses this *1800-foot-tall peak* to symbolize majesty. In Jeremiah 46:18, he wrote, "'As I live,' declares the King whose name is the LORD of hosts, 'Surely one shall come who looms up like Tabor among the mountains, or like Carmel by the sea'" **(NASB)**.

◆ Because some traditions say the transfiguration happened on Mount Tabor,

a church was constructed there 1,500 years ago. That church is no longer there—but one built about 100 years ago, **the Basilica of the Transfiguration**, can still be seen.

◆ **Hiking** is also available at Mount Tabor. One route goes up the mountain, and another goes around the base. From Mount Tabor, one can see Nazareth and Galilee.

34

NAZARETH

Nazareth, home village of Mary and site of the annunciation. Joseph and Mary resettled in Nazareth after returning from their flight from Bethlehem to Egypt. Jesus spent his childhood in Nazareth.
(Terry Bidgood / ODBM)

*The crowds answered, "This is Jesus, the prophet from **Nazareth** in Galilee."*

MATTHEW 21:11

WHERE TO FIND IT IN THE BIBLE

Matthew 2:23; 4:13; 21:11; 26:71; Mark 1:9, 24; 10:47; Luke 1:26; 2:4, 39, 51; 4:14, 16, 34; 18:37; 24:19; John 1:45–46; 18:5, 7; 19:19; Acts 2:22; 3:6; 4:10

KEY PASSAGES ABOUT NAZARETH

❝ In the sixth month of Elizabeth's pregnancy, God sent the angel

Gabriel to Nazareth, a town in Galilee. (LUKE 1:26)

66 [Jesus] went and lived in a town called Nazareth. So was fulfilled what was said through the prophets that he would be called a Nazarene. (MATTHEW 2:23)

66 Jesus came from Nazareth in Galilee and was baptized by John in the Jordan. (MARK 1:9)

66 Philip found Nathanael and told him, "We have found the one Moses wrote about in the Law, and about whom the prophets also wrote—Jesus of Nazareth, the son of Joseph." "Nazareth! Can anything good come from there?" Nathanael asked. (JOHN 1:45–46)

66 Pilate had a notice prepared and fastened to the cross. It read: JESUS OF NAZARETH, THE KING OF THE JEWS. (JOHN 19:19)

66 Know this, you and all the people of Israel: It is by the name of Jesus Christ of Nazareth, whom you crucified but whom God raised from the dead, that this man stands before you healed. (ACTS 4:10)

BIBLE STUFF THAT HAPPENED AT NAZARETH

● In Nazareth, the angel Gabriel made the amazing announcement that Mary would give birth to the Messiah Jesus.

● Mary and Joseph took Jesus as a young boy to Nazareth after they had spent time in Egypt escaping the murderous threats of Herod.

● After Jesus's family had traveled to Jerusalem for Passover, their family group headed back home. On that journey, Mary and Joseph noticed that Jesus was not in their group. After going back to Jerusalem and finding Him teaching in the synagogue,

Over the entrance to the Church of the Annunciation is carved the Latin phrasing of this verse: "The Word was made flesh, and dwelt among us" (JOHN 1:14 KJV). (Terry Bidgood / ODBM)

146

Terry Bidgood / ODBM

NAZARETH TODAY

Today the city of Nazareth, the largest Arab city in Israel, has a population of about 77,000 people. It is a bustling, business-driven city that is nothing like the pastoral village we might envision. Yet it still has several interesting sites with biblical connections.

they trekked back to Nazareth. There Jesus obeyed His parents (**LUKE 2:51**) and Mary treasured "all these things in her heart. And Jesus grew in wisdom and stature, and in favor with God and man" (**V. 52**) for the remainder of His life in Nazareth.

WHERE TO FIND IT IN ISRAEL

Far to the north of Jerusalem, yet parallel and west of the southern tip of the Sea of Galilee stands Nazareth. The distance is about ninety miles. In Jesus's day Nazareth was "an insignificant village in a hollow in the Galilean hills."[14] (**SEE MAP ON PAGE 142.**)

THINGS TO SEE

◆ *Church of the Annunciation:* Its architecture dominates Nazareth, and its history spans 1,600 years. After having been built and destroyed four times over the centuries, the current building that reflects the angel's visit with Mary was built in the mid 1900s.

◆ *Mary's Well:* The traditional site of the well from which Mary would have drawn water can be seen in Nazareth.

◆ *Jesus's House?* An archaeological site that has been explored since the 1800s took on new significance in 2006 when expert Ken Dark proposed that the site, which is comprised of ruins of ancient homes, could very well have been Jesus's boyhood home. This can be found inside the Mary of Nazareth International Center.

PHILIPPI

*From [Neapolis] [Paul and others] traveled to **Philippi**, a Roman colony and the leading city of that district of Macedonia.* ACTS 16:12

WHERE TO FIND IT IN THE BIBLE

Acts 16:11–12; 20:6; Philippians 1:1; 4:15; 1 Thessalonians 2:2

KEY PASSAGES ABOUT PHILIPPI

❝ Paul and Timothy, servants of Christ Jesus, to all God's holy people in Christ Jesus at Philippi, together with the overseers and deacons. **(PHILIPPIANS 1:1)**

❝ We had previously suffered and been treated outrageously in Philippi, as you know, but with the help of our God we dared to tell you his gospel in the face of strong opposition. **(1 THESSALONIANS 2:2)**

BIBLE STUFF THAT HAPPENED AT PHILIPPI

Because the Holy Spirit directed Paul to go to Macedonia, he ventured to Philippi, and as a

Ruins of ancient **Philippi**, looking northwest along the portico (stoa) of the city's main marketplace (or agora). In the distance (at right) is visible the acropolis, or high hill, of the city. (Ian W. Scott / Creative Commons)

result Philippi is the first European city that heard the gospel.

Paul was visiting Troas on the western tip of Asia. He had a vision of a man of Macedonia begging him to "Come over to Macedonia and help us" (ACTS 16:9). The next day, he and his traveling companions got on a ship that sailed first to the island of Samothrace and then on to Neopolis on the east coast of northern Greece (Macedonia). They then took the Roman trade route (the Via Egnatia) to Philippi. The Via Egnatia ran right through the middle of Philippi. In this town Lydia, a woman who sold purple cloth, became the city's first Christian under Paul's ministry.

Paul got himself into trouble in Philippi

Above: Floor mosaic with the name of St. Paul in the Octagonal Basilica (circa 343) (Berthold Werner / Creative Commons). *Right:* A Greek open-air theater excavated in the 1920s (XeresNelro / Creative Commons).

for casting an evil spirit out of a little girl. This caused financial hardship for the owners of this slave girl, who had been using her ability to predict the future as a way to make money. Paul and his friend Silas were thrown into jail for the trouble they caused. They were miraculously released from prison.

Through the conversion of Lydia and others, the first European Christian church was established in Philippi. Paul never returned to Philippi, but the people supported him in his work. And, of course, he wrote a letter that became the biblical

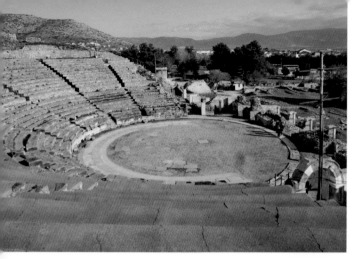

book of Philippians. They received his letter in the early AD 60s.

WHERE TO FIND IT IN EUROPE

The ancient city of Philippi is in the north-eastern section of Greece. The modern town of Filippoi is nearby.

The remains of Philippi can be reached via bus from the cities of Kaval and Drama. Visitors to Philippi can walk among the ruins.

THINGS TO SEE

◆ Three of the **city's gates**, which were part of the security perimeter for Philippi, can still be seen.

◆ A **Roman open-air theater** that was built after Paul's time has been discovered.

◆ The supposed place where Paul was jailed. While it has not been verified as the actual jail where Paul and Silas were imprisoned, it can give the visitor the idea of **a first-century jail** in Philippi.

◆ The **agora**, which was the marketplace.

◆ The ruins of what is believed to be **the first Christian church**. It is believed to have been dedicated (according to an inscription on a discovered mosaic) to Paul.

◆ Remnants of the **Via Egnatia**. Back in the days of Paul, this major road ran from Rome to Asia Minor—a distance of more than five hundred miles. A portion of this road can still be seen in Philippi.

PHILIPPI TODAY

The ancient city of Philippi was abandoned in the fourteenth century. Its ruins have been excavated by archaeologists since the early twentieth century. Today it is a UNESCO World Heritage site.

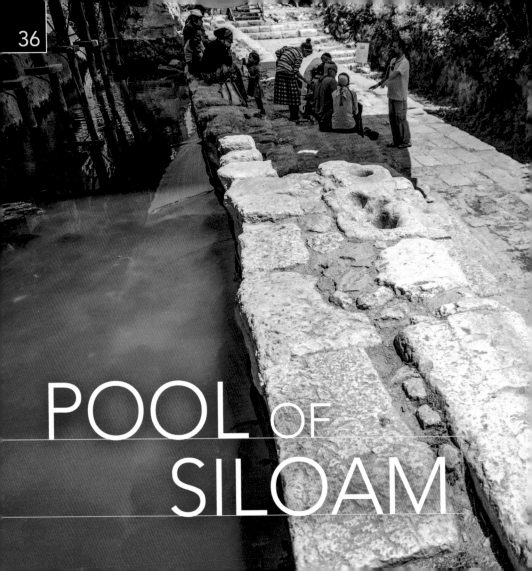

36

POOL of SILOAM

Terry Bidgood / ODBM

> *"Go," he told him, "wash in the **Pool of Siloam**" (this word means "Sent"). So the man went and washed, and came home seeing.* JOHN 9:7

WHERE TO FIND IT IN THE BIBLE

Nehemiah 3:15; John 9:1–41

KEY PASSAGES ABOUT THE POOL OF SILOAM

❝ The Fountain Gate was repaired by Shallun son of Kol-Hozeh, ruler of the district of Mizpah. He rebuilt it, roofing it over and putting its doors and bolts and bars in place. He also repaired the wall of the Pool of Siloam, by the King's Garden, as far as the steps going down from the City of David. **(NEHEMIAH 3:15)**

❝ [Jesus] spit on the ground, made some mud with the saliva, and put it on the man's eyes. "Go," he told him, "wash in the Pool of Siloam" (this word means "Sent"). **(JOHN 9:6–7)**

BIBLE STUFF THAT HAPPENED AT THE POOL

The Pool of Siloam appears just three times in the Bible. In the Old Testament, we see the repair of the pool in Nehemiah 3, and in the New Testament it is mentioned twice in John 9 when Jesus healed a man born blind.

WHERE TO FIND IT IN ISRAEL

According to the *Archaeology Study Bible,* visitors to Jerusalem were for hundreds of years shown the wrong pool. In the early part of the twenty-first century, workers discovered another pool that researchers are now convinced is the real Pool of Siloam. Artifacts found at the more recently discovered location matched the time period of Jesus. The Pool of Siloam is located outside of Jerusalem southeast of the Temple Mount. It is just west of the Kidron Valley.

THINGS TO SEE

Visitors to the Pool of Siloam (signs refer to it as the Shiloah Pool) will not see the actual pool, for it has not been excavated due to digging restrictions. What one sees there are the steps that go down into the pool, which itself is underneath a garden.

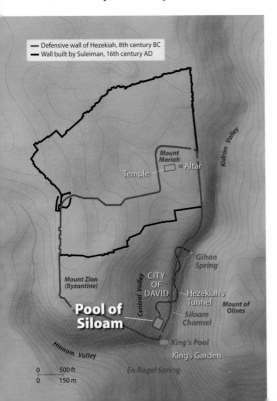

- Defensive wall of Hezekiah, 8th century BC
- Wall built by Suleiman, 16th century AD

Mount Moriah

Temple

Altar

Kidron Valley

Gihon Spring

Mount Zion (Byzantine)

Central Valley

CITY OF DAVID

Hezekiah's Tunnel

Mount of Olives

Siloam Channel

Pool of Siloam

King's Pool

Hinnom Valley

King's Garden

En Rogel Spring

0   500 ft
0   150 m

The Pool of Siloam—a rock-cut pool—is situated on the southern slope of the City of David, the original site Jerusalem, located outside the walls of the Old City to the southeast. The pool was fed by the waters of Gihon Spring. (Abraham / Public domain)

SEA OF

*As Jesus was walking beside the **Sea of Galilee**, he saw two brothers, Simon called Peter and his brother Andrew. They were casting a net into the lake, for they were fishermen. "Come, follow me," Jesus said.*

MATTHEW 4:18–19

37

WHERE TO FIND IT IN THE BIBLE

Matthew 4:18; John 6:1; 21:1
"Lake" for Sea of Galilee:
Matthew 8:24, 32; 14:25–26; 17:27

KEY PASSAGES ABOUT THE SEA OF GALILEE

❝ Suddenly a furious storm came up on the lake, so that the waves swept over the boat. **(MATTHEW 8:24)**

❝ Jesus left [Tyre and Sidon] and went along the Sea of Galilee.

GALILEE

The Sea of Galilee is the lowest freshwater lake on Earth at nearly seven hundred feet below sea level. It is fed by underground springs and the Jordan River from the north.

Then he went up on a mountainside and sat down. **(MATTHEW 15:29)**

BIBLE STUFF THAT HAPPENED AT THE SEA OF GALILEE

- Jesus picked Peter and Andrew.
- Jesus walked on the water.
- Jesus calmed the storm.
- Jesus sent pigs into the lake.
- Jesus taught by the Sea of Galilee.
- Jesus fed the thousands near the Sea of Galilee.
- Jesus appeared to some disciples by the Sea of Galilee after His resurrection.

WHERE TO FIND IT IN ISRAEL

The most notable city on the Sea of Galilee (also called Kinneret) is Tiberias on the lake's western shore. (Tiberias is mentioned in **JOHN 6:23**. Boats from

Left: Kursi is an archaeological site containing the ruins of a Byzantine monastery and identified by tradition as the site of Jesus's "Miracle of the Swine" on the eastern side of the Sea of Galilee (Stephanie Gottschalk / Pixabay.com). *Right:* Church of the Primacy of Saint Peter, supposed site of Simon Peter's restoration by Jesus after the resurrection (Berthold Werner / Public domain).

FAVORITE SITE REFLECTION

I wrote in my journal while visiting Israel: "Coming over the hill, as I looked to the left and glimpsed for the first time the Sea of Galilee, an emotion struck that is indescribable—a feeling of true kinship to the Savior. A breathtaking reality. He was there, and now I was there. Where Jesus walked on the water— and now I was seeing that water! A lifetime of familiar terms suddenly became real." It was among the

Terry Bidgood / ODBM

most emotional moments while visiting the Holy Land—seeing for the first time this body of water that was so crucial to Jesus's ministry.

Tiberias had landed near where Jesus had been, and the people were looking for Him.) Traveling from Jerusalem to Tiberias takes a little over two hours (about 115 miles). **(SEE MAP ON PAGE 142.)**

THINGS TO SEE

◆ *The Sea* itself. The Sea of Galilee stretches thirteen miles north to south and nine miles east to west. It is dotted with beaches and recreation spots.

◆ Sites of biblical importance such as *Capernaum, Magdala,* and *Bethsaida* ring the Sea.

◆ It is possible to take *boat tours* on the Sea—to give the visitor an idea of what Jesus and His disciples experienced. Kayaks can be rented for a more physical trip on the Sea.

38

SHECHEM

Judges 9:1–4 mentions the "house of Baal-berith,"
a temple to Baal. This archaeological dig in Shechem (or
Nablus) most probably contains the ruins of that temple.
(Ibrahim Dwaikat / Creative Commons)

*After Jacob came from Paddan Aram, he arrived safely at the city of **Shechem** in Canaan and camped within sight of the city. For a hundred pieces of silver, he bought from the sons of Hamor, the father of Shechem, the plot of ground where he pitched his tent. There he set up an altar and called it El Elohe Israel.*

GENESIS 33:18–20

WHERE TO FIND IT IN THE BIBLE

Genesis 33:19; 35:4; 37:13–14; Joshua 17:2, 7; 21:21; 24:1, 25, 32; Judges 9:1–4, 6–7, 18, 20, 23–26; Acts 7:16

KEY PASSAGE ABOUT SHECHEM

❝ Abram traveled through the land as far as the site of the great tree of Moreh at Shechem. **(GENESIS 12:6)**

BIBLE STUFF THAT HAPPENED AT SHECHEM

● After Abram was told by God to leave Ur, he settled first in Haran for many years. When he left to go to Canaan, his first recorded stop was at Shechem. Abram built an altar to the Lord there.

● Next on the scene was Jacob. He camped within sight of the city of Shechem, and he spent one hundred pieces of silver to buy the land where he pitched his tent (**GENESIS 33:18–20**). He, like Abram, built an altar on this land.

● Joseph's brothers were near Shechem tending the family flocks when Jacob sent Joseph to check on his brothers. (**GENESIS 37:12–14**).

● At Shechem, Joshua "assembled all the tribes of Israel" (**JOSHUA 24:1**). He then rehearsed for the people everything God had

Above: The city of Nablus (Shechem) with Mount Eba to the right and Mount Gerizim to the left (Uwe a / Creat Commons). *Below:* Tell Balata, the site thought to be anc Shechem. The area is part of Tell Balata Archaeologic Park. The park's guidebook can be accessed online a unesdoc.unesco.org (Dr. Avishai Teicher / Creative Commons).

done for them, and he asked the people if they would make a covenant to serve God.

They said, "We too will serve the LORD" (JOSHUA 24:18).

● Joshua set up a stone of remembrance "under the oak" at Shechem (GENESIS 35:4).

● Joseph's bones were eventually buried at Shechem. The Israelites carried his body from Egypt.

WHERE TO FIND IT IN ISRAEL

About midway between the Sea of Galilee and the Dead Sea—and then inland from the Jordan River—stands Shechem. It is about thirty miles north of Jerusalem. The city is located in a pass between two peaks: Mount Ebal and Mount Gerizim. (SEE MAP ON PAGE 10.)

THINGS TO SEE

One of the most important promises by the people of Israel was made in Shechem. Although there is not much left to see of the ancient city, one can see the topography of the land and get a better impression of what went on as recorded at the end of the book of Joshua. The city sits at the bottom of two mountain peaks: Ebal and Gerizim. It was there that the people promised: "We will serve the LORD!"

◆ **Gate from Jacob's time:** At Shechem, visitors can see a small section of the protection from the days of Jacob. The stone-made foundations of the gate can still be seen. It is possible that they were in use during the time of Abimelech.

◆ **Tell Balata:** This archaeological site is surrounded by the modern city of Shechem. This archaeological dig revealed a tomb called Joseph's Tomb.

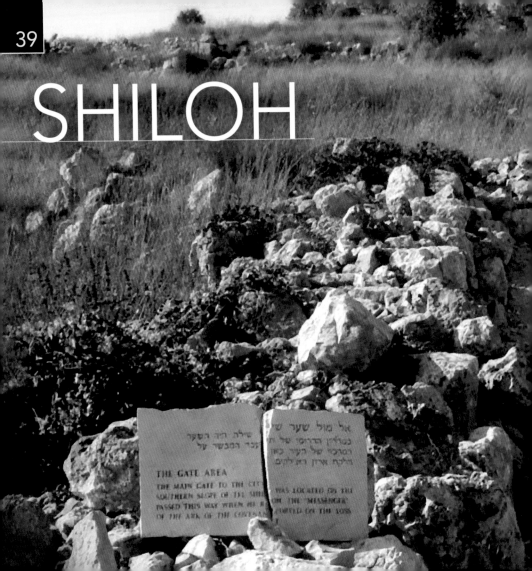

SHILOH

אל מול שער שי
נמצאין הדרומי של ח
המרכזי של העיר כא
הלכה ארון ברית לחם

שילת תיד השער
וגבד המבשר על

THE GATE AREA
THE MAIN GATE TO THE CIT... ...WAS LOCATED ON THE
SOUTHERN SLOPE OF THE SHIL... ...ON THE "MIAMBGER"
PASSED THIS WAY WHEN HE R... ...PORTED ON THE LOSS
OF THE ARK OF THE COVENANT...

*The whole assembly of the Israelites gathered at **Shiloh** and set up the tent of meeting there.*

JOSHUA 18:1

WHERE TO FIND IT IN THE BIBLE

Joshua 18:1, 8, 10; 22:12; Judges 18:31; 21:19; 1 Samuel 1:3, 9, 24; 3:21; 4:4; 1 Kings 2:27; 14:2; Psalm 78:60; Jeremiah 7:12; 26:6

KEY PASSAGES ABOUT SHILOH

❝ Joshua then cast lots for them in Shiloh in the presence of the LORD, and there he distributed the land to the Israelites according to their tribal divisions. **(JOSHUA 18:10)**

❝ The whole assembly of Israel gathered at Shiloh to go to war against them. **(JOSHUA 22:12)**

❝ They continued to use the idol Micah had made, all the time the house of God was in Shiloh. **(JUDGES 18:31)**

❝ Year after year this man went up from his

Shiloh Trail: This engraved stone reads, "The main gate to the city was located on the southern slope of the Tel Shiloh. The 'messenger' passed this way when he reported on the loss of the ark of the covenant." (Peace House / Creative Commons)

town to worship and sacrifice to the LORD Almighty at Shiloh, where Hophni and Phinehas, the two sons of Eli, were priests of the LORD. **(1 SAMUEL 1:3)**

❝ After he was weaned, she took the boy with her, young as he was, along with a three-year-old bull, an ephah of flour and a skin of wine, and brought him to the house of the LORD at Shiloh. **(1 SAMUEL 1:24)**

❝ Then I will make this house like Shiloh and this city a curse among all the nations of the earth. **(JEREMIAH 26:6)**

BIBLE STUFF THAT HAPPENED AT SHILOH

● After the children of Israel crossed the Jordan River to establish themselves in the promised land, Shiloh became their first worship center before the temple was built. The tabernacle, which the Israelites had taken with them on their wilderness

Above: A model of the Altar of the Mishkan at Tel Shiloh, based on biblical references (Yair Aronshtam / Creative Commons).
Left: The hills and ravines believed to be the site of ancient Shiloh (aliv g / Creative Commons).

WHERE TO FIND IT IN ISRAEL

Judges 21:19 tells us exactly where Shiloh was located: "north of Bethel, east of the road that goes from Bethel to Shechem, and south of Lebonah." That description still stands, for the ruins of Shiloh are midway between Bethel and Shechem. Also, by today's reckoning, it is about twenty miles north of Jerusalem. Today, it is known as Khirbet Seilun, and it can be found in southern Samaria. **(SEE MAP ON PAGE 38.)**

trek, was given a more permanent home in Shiloh.

● It was in Shiloh that Joshua divvied out the land to the tribes.

● Hannah prayed for a son, and he was born to her at Shiloh. And he was dedicated to the Lord's service at Shiloh.

● After the ark of the covenant was taken from Shiloh by Eli's sons, the tabernacle was abandoned **(PSALM 78:60)**, and the city was no longer a worship center. Jeremiah spoke of Shiloh in a negative context because the tabernacle had been destroyed **(JEREMIAH 7:12–14; 26:4–9).**

THINGS TO SEE

The old city of Shiloh, of course, is gone. It was destroyed by the Philistines in the eleventh century BC. However, modern archaeological excavations allow us to get a glimpse of life in Shiloh in its various eras. Among the finds at Shiloh have been Bronze Age artifacts (before 1500 BC). Even then, religious activity was evident in Shiloh, mostly by the Canaanites and before the conquest by the Israelites.

40

*King Solomon also built a **palace** for himself; it took him thirteen years to finish it.* **1 KINGS 7:1 (NCV)**

WHERE TO FIND IT IN THE BIBLE

1 Kings 3:1; 7:1–2; 9:10; 10:21; 2 Chronicles 8:1; 9:20

KEY PASSAGES ABOUT SOLOMON'S PALACE

❝ Solomon made an alliance with Pharaoh king of Egypt and married his daughter. He brought her to the City of David until he finished building his palace. **(1 KINGS 3:1)**

❝ At the end of twenty years, during which Solomon built these two buildings—the temple of the Lord and the royal palace. **(1 KINGS 9:10)**

NOTE: During Solomon's time, other palaces were built in locations other than

An excavated Jerusalem site includes a wall that archaeologist Dr. Eilat Mazar says is likely to have been built by the biblical King Solomon. Ancient artifacts found there are dated to the tenth-century BC. (Alex Soh / ODBM)

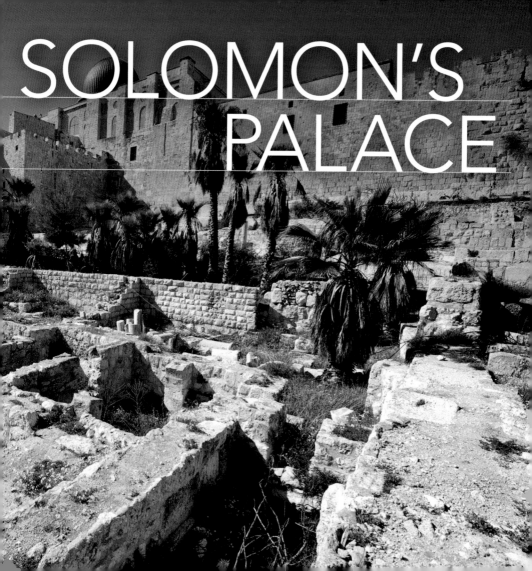

SOLOMON'S PALACE

Jerusalem, and they are referred to as Solomon's palaces. One of those buildings was discovered by archaeologists at Gezer.

BIBLE STUFF THAT HAPPENED AT KING SOLOMON'S PALACE

A reading of the description of Solomon's palace in 1 Kings 7 reveals some of the activities in that building:

● There was a throne hall, so we can assume that Solomon presided over events in that hall from a throne.

● There was a Hall of Justice, which is perhaps where he made his ruling about the two women who both claimed to be the mother of the same baby.

● The living quarters included a separate palace for his wife who was Pharaoh's daughter.

● Among the implements in the palace were golden shields, golden goblets, plus harps and lyres for the musicians (**1 KINGS 10**).

● It appears that the Queen of Sheba visited Solomon's palace (**1 KINGS 10:4**).

● During the reign of King Rehoboam, "Shishak king of Egypt attacked Jerusalem. He carried off the treasures of the temple of the LORD and the treasures of the royal palace" (including the gold shields). (**SEE 1 KINGS 14:25–26**).

WHERE TO FIND IT IN ISRAEL

In about 2010, Israeli archaeologist Eilat Mazar discovered what she is confident is the partial remains of Solomon's palace. She discovered a wall that she is convinced was built during Solomon's time. Using pottery and other evidences, Mazar is convinced the wall was part of the structure for Solomon's complex, including the palace. It

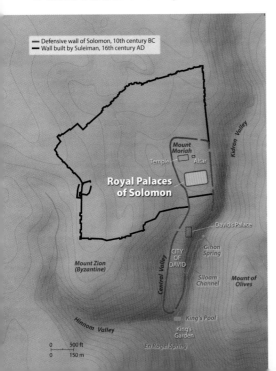

— Defensive wall of Solomon, 10th century BC
— Wall built by Suleiman, 16th century AD

Mount Moriah
Temple   Altar
Kidron Valley
Royal Palaces of Solomon
David's Palace
Gihon Spring
CITY OF DAVID
Mount Zion (Byzantine)
Central Valley
Siloam Channel
Mount of Olives
Hinnom Valley
King's Pool
King's Garden
En Rogel Spring
0   500 ft
0   150 m

Temple Mount aerial view, southeast exposure. The red outline is the approximate area of Dr. Eilat Mazar's recent dig which revealed a small portion of Solomon's royal complex. (Andrew Shiva / Creative Commons)

is located at the southern end of the Temple Mount—a place that until not too long ago was unexcavated. Visitors can take tours of this archaeological site, which is called the Ophel Archaeological Park. It is located near the Western Wall in the Old City.

THINGS TO SEE

At this location is the **Davidson Center**, which houses a museum. In the museum are numerous artifacts discovered during archaeological excavations.

41

TEMPLE
MOUNT

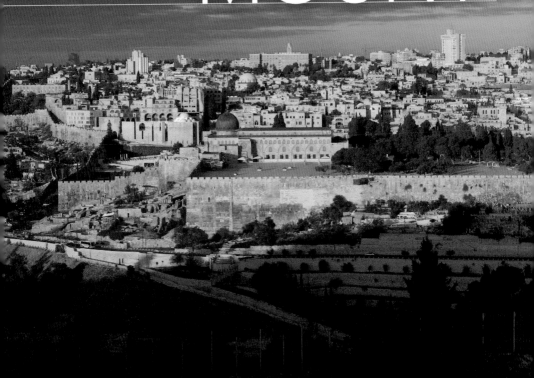

Each day Jesus was teaching at the temple, and each evening he went out to spend the night on the hill called the Mount of Olives, and all the people came early in the morning to hear him at the temple. **LUKE 21:37–38**

WHERE TO FIND IT IN THE BIBLE

The term **temple mount** is not found in the Bible, but we can find many references to things that happened at this amazing location in Jerusalem: Genesis 22:2; 2 Samuel 24:18–25; 1 Kings 5–6; 2 Chronicles 3:1; Matthew 24:1–2; Luke 2:22–38, 41–51; John 2:14–16

KEY PASSAGES ABOUT TEMPLE MOUNT

❝ Then God said, "Take your son, your only son, whom you love—Isaac—and go to the region of Moriah. Sacrifice him there as a burnt offering on a mountain I will show you." **(GENESIS 22:2)**

❝ Araunah said, "Why has my lord the king come to his servant?" "To buy your threshing floor," David answered, "so I can build an altar to the LORD." **(2 SAMUEL 24:21)**

❝ Then Solomon began to build the temple of the LORD in Jerusalem on Mount Moriah. **(2 CHRONICLES 3:1)**

❝ Jesus left the temple and was walking away when

he **Temple Mount** is a trapezoid-shaped, walled-in area in the outheastern corner of the Old City Jerusalem. Some of the four walls ate back to the time of the Second wish Temple, built at the end of st century BC. (WerkstattRU / Pixabay.com)

173

his disciples came up to him to call his attention to its buildings. "Do you see all these things?" he asked. "Truly I tell you, not one stone here will be left on another; every one will be thrown down."
(MATTHEW 24:1–2)

BIBLE STUFF THAT HAPPENED AT THE TEMPLE MOUNT

● Some religious traditions believe the Temple Mount is actually Mount Moriah, where Abraham was prepared to sacrifice Isaac before God provided an animal substitute.

● The site of the temple was at one time a threshing floor.

● Solomon built his temple here, and it stood for about four hundred years—until it was destroyed by the Babylonians in about 587 BC. When the exiled Jews were allowed to return to Jerusalem, they rebuilt the temple, completing it in 515 BC. King Herod remodeled and refurbished it into a grand temple in the first century BC. In 70 AD, Romans destroyed the second temple.

● When Jesus's parents were returning to Nazareth after Passover, they discovered that Jesus was not with them. Upon their return to Jerusalem to look for Him, they found Him in the temple, teaching the elders. He was twelve at the time.

● Jesus entered the temple area and overturned the tables of the money changers, who were desecrating the area with their greed.

WHERE TO FIND IT IN ISRAEL

The view of the Temple Mount from the Mount of Olives is one of the most iconic sites in the world. Dominated by the Dome of the Rock, it is seen best from the Mount of Olives. The Temple Mount is the spot from which a visitor to Jerusalem gets his bearings because it dominates the landscape.

THINGS TO SEE

NOTE: There are dress codes that must be followed for all who enter the Temple Mount. For instance, no shorts are allowed. Dress must be modest.

◆ Entrance to the Temple Mount is through the **Moors' Gate**, or sometimes called the Mughrabi Gate. It is just to the south of the Wailing Wall.

◆ **The Dome of the Rock.** This is an Islamic shrine that was constructed in the AD 600s. While non-Muslims cannot enter the shrine, visitors of all faiths can get a close-up look while walking on the Temple Mount. It was built on the

Terry Bidgood / ODBM

FAVORITE SITE REFLECTION

There is a certain peacefulness that surrounds the area of the Temple Mount. Perhaps it is because it stands above the noise and bustle of the city. Perhaps it is because of the understood aura of being in a spot revered by three of the world's largest religions. But I think it was more than that. Similar to the Sea of Galilee, this area evokes thoughts of the Prince of Peace. In quiet moments of contemplation, one can imagine twelve-year-old Jesus on this very spot impressing the religious leaders with His wisdom. And for pure excitement, one can think of an angry Jesus appearing twenty-one years later to cleanse the temple area of greedy money changers. I picked up a tiny remembrance of the Mount—a very small rock. It has no intrinsic meaning, but it helps me think back to an era long ago when our Savior walked this same area.

supposed site of the second temple. Jews in Jerusalem have begun plans to build a third temple on the mount.

◆ The Western Wall of the Temple Mount is what is often called the **Wailing Wall.** It is actually a foundational wall from the Temple Mount left over from the first century. This is a sacred spot for Jews, who can be found worshiping and praying at this wall.

TEMPLE MOUNT TODAY

The Temple Mount is a sacred spot for Muslims, Jews, and Christians alike. Entrance to the area is controlled by Muslims and sometimes a passport is required for entrance. Christians and Jews are usually not allowed to pray on the Temple Mount or conduct any kind of religious activities, but it has happened in recent years.

42

THESSALONI

Thessalonica (now Thessaloniki) is located on the Thermaic Gulf, at the northwest corner of the Aegean Sea. It has a population of more than one million residents.
(Dimitris Vetsikas / Pixabay.com)

*When [Paul and Silas] had passed through Amphipolis and Apollonia, they came to **Thessalonica**, where there was a Jewish synagogue.* ACTS 17:1

CA

WHERE TO FIND IT IN THE BIBLE

Acts 17:1, 11, 13; 20:4; 27:2; Philippians 4:16; 1 Thessalonians 1:1; 2 Timothy 4:10

KEY PASSAGES ABOUT THESSALONICA

❝ When [Paul and Silas] had passed through Amphipolis and Apollonia, they came to Thessalonica, where there was a Jewish synagogue. **(ACTS 17:1)**

> **To the church of the Thessalonians in God the Father and the Lord Jesus Christ: Grace and peace to you.**
> **(1 THESSALONIANS 1:1)**

BIBLE STUFF THAT HAPPENED AT THESSALONICA

● Paul and Silas arrived in Thessalonica after they were asked to leave Philippi by the city officials.

● Paul preached in the synagogue in Thessalonica for three Sabbaths, and he was able to persuade many people to put their faith in Jesus.

● The Jews in Thessalonica were outraged by this, so they went looking for Paul and Silas. The crowds went to the home of a man named Jason, assuming Paul and Silas would be there. They weren't. Jason had to post bond to free himself from the mob.

● Paul referred to his aborted trip to Thessalonica in his first letter to them, contending that his trip there "was not without results" (1 THESSALONIANS 2:1).

● Paul wanted to return to Thessalonica but "Satan stopped us," he wrote to the church there (1 THESSALONIANS 2:18 TLB).

WHERE TO FIND IT IN GREECE

Like Philippi, Thessalonica was a city on the Via Egnatia. Unlike Philippi, it

Above: This mosaic in a late fifth-century church (Hosios David) in Thessalonica depicts the theophany of Christ holding a Greek text saying, "Behold our God, in whom we hope and we rejoice in our salvation, that he may grant rest to this home" (Mboesch / Creative Commons). *Right:* **The Church of St. Demetrius**, originally built in the fourth century (ActFree / Creative Commons, Public domain). *Far right:* A section of the **Via Egnatia** in Kavala, Greece, east of Thessalonica (Philipp Pilhofer / Creative Commons).

still exists today in modern form—not just in archaeological digs. It is located west of Philippi along the coast of the Aegean Sea. The city today is called either Thessaloniki or Salonica. The Via Egnatia, which in Philippi is an ancient, unused road, is the name of a busy four-lane highway that runs through the city of more than 300,000 people (whether this is the actual route of the original Via Egnatia is under debate).

THINGS TO SEE

◆ Because the city has continued to exist over the past two thousand years, little is left to remind visitors of the days when Paul and Silas visited. Some excavations have revealed some first-century sites, such as a **bathhouse**. A **gate** that dates back to the first century was discovered to have an inscription that used the word "politarches," which was the term for city officials that Luke used to describe the people who questioned Jason about Paul and Silas (**ACTS 17:6**). Other Roman-era finds include a **palace** and the **Roman forum**.

◆ Two churches of interest are the **Agia Sophia** and the **Church of St. Demetrius**. Neither are first-century churches nor do they have direct connection to Paul's visit—other than that Paul had introduced Christianity to the city, and it continued to be influential. The Church of St. Demetrius was built in the fourth century and reconstructed in the sixth century after a fire. The Agia Sophia is a model of the original church of the same name in Constantinople. The one in Greece was built in the seventh century.

THESSALONICA TODAY

Thessaloniki is the second-largest city in Greece today. According to the website greeka.com, the country is 98 percent Christian Orthodox,[15] which would indicate a similar distribution in Thessaloniki.

43

TIBERIAS

*Then some boats from **Tiberias** landed near the place where the people had eaten the bread after the Lord had given thanks.*

JOHN 6:23

The biblical town of **Rakkath** (established around 1200 BC) eventually became present-day **Tiberias**, a city on the western shore of the Sea of Galilee. Established around AD 20, Tiberias was named in honor of the second emperor of the Roman Empire. (Tiberias municipality / Creative Commons)

WHERE TO FIND IT IN THE BIBLE

Joshua 19:35, John 6:23

KEY PASSAGES ABOUT TIBERIAS

❝ The fortified cities were Ziddim, Zer, Hammath, Rakkath, Kinnereth, Adamah, Ramah, Hazor... **(JOSHUA 19:35–36)**

(**NOTE:** Rakkath is very near the location of Tiberias, built in the first century AD.)

❝ Then some boats from Tiberias landed near the place where the people had eaten the bread after the Lord had given thanks. **(JOHN 6:23)**

BIBLE STUFF THAT HAPPENED AT TIBERIAS

● Although Tiberias is mentioned just once in Scripture by its actual name **(JOHN 6:23)** and once by an earlier name from the area **(JOSHUA 19:35)**, it has enough interest related to the Bible story and its aftermath to warrant a visit.

● The Joshua mention was of a town named Rakkath, which was a fortified (or walled) city in the territory populated by the Naphtali tribe of Israelites.

Jewish tradition says that the city of Tiberias was built in the same location as this ancient Naphtalian town.

● The city of Tiberias had been established by the first century, for John 6 tells us that followers of Jesus hired boats from Tiberias to make the trip to the east side

Above: Looking east from the Galilean shore at Tiberias (Heather Truett, Pixabay.com).
Right: On the northern end of Tiberias is the mound of Tel Rakkat (R. Hartov / Public domain).
Far right: Fish and chips, Tiberias-style, includes "St. Peter's fish," redbelly tilapia. (Etan Tal / Creative Commons).

of the Sea of Galilee in search of Jesus. Not finding Him there, the people took the boats to Capernaum as they sought Him.

WHERE TO FIND IT IN ISRAEL

The closest route from Jerusalem to Tiberias takes a bit less than two hours. Take Route 50 out of Jerusalem and connect with Route 1 heading north. Connect with Route 6 north to Route 70 and then 77 into Tiberias.

Tiberias is on the western shore of the Sea of Galilee about midway between its

northernmost and southernmost tips.

There is public transportation available (bus) from Jerusalem to Tiberias, but no trains. **(SEE MAP ON PAGE 22.)**

THINGS TO SEE

◆ *Tel Rakkat:* This is a mound just west of the Sea of Galilee and adjacent to the road that goes along the Sea. It can be climbed by visitors, but there is no archaeological excavating going on currently.

◆ *St. Peter's Restaurant:* While this is not specifically related to anything biblical in the archaeological sense, diners do get to imagine first-century eating. Order the St. Peter's fish and imagine Jesus and His disciples eating this fish on the shore at the breakfast Jesus served, or imagine being one of the 5,000 fed by Jesus from the fish in the boy's lunch.

Tel Rakkat

44

WILDERNESS TEMPTATION

Of the Judean Wilderness, where Jesus was tempted by Satan, Dr. Jack Beck says, "The Spirit led Jesus into the wilderness, . . . so he could face 'temptation' in the same type of setting as the Israelites."[16] (Alex Soh / ODBM)

*Then Jesus was led by the Spirit into the **wilderness** to be tempted by the devil.* **MATTHEW 4:1**

OF

WHERE TO FIND IT IN THE BIBLE

Matthew 4:1–4;
Mark 1:12–13; Luke 4:1–4

KEY PASSAGES ABOUT THE TEMPTATION OF JESUS

❝ Then Jesus was led by the Spirit into the wilderness to be tempted by the devil. After fasting forty days and forty nights, he was hungry. The tempter came to him. **(MATTHEW 4:1–4)**

❝ At once the Spirit sent him out into the wilderness, and he was in the wilderness forty days, being tempted by Satan. He was with the wild animals, and angels attended him. **(MARK 1:12–13)**

❝ Jesus, full of the Holy Spirit, left the Jordan and was led by the Spirit into the wilderness, where for forty days he was tempted by the devil. **(LUKE 4:1–2)**

BIBLE STUFF THAT HAPPENED IN THE WILDERNESS

After His baptism, Jesus was led by the Holy Spirit into the Judean Wilderness. There He fasted for forty days and was in the neighborhood of wild animals **(MARK 1:13)**. It was there that Satan met with Jesus and tested Him with three temptations that Jesus overcame using Scripture **(LUKE 4:1–13)**.

WHERE TO FIND IT IN ISRAEL

In the Judean Wilderness is an outcropping called Mount Guarantania. This is the traditional location of Jesus's temptation. In Luke 4:5, we read that "the devil led him up to a high place," which may be that mountain. It is located less than five miles from Jericho. Visitors can visit the top of the mountain by a walking tour up a path.

Left: **Jebel Quarantal** viewed from an ancient excavation site in Jericho. To the left the cable car installation can be seen which leads right up to the mount's monastery (Ayoshust / Creative Commons). *Above:* Jack Beck exploring a road into the barren **Judean Wilderness** (Terry Bidgood / ODBM).

tells us. Here is Dr. Jack Beck concerning the location: "Since John was preaching in the Judean Wilderness **(MATTHEW 3:1)** and Jesus was baptized opposite Jericho near Bethany Beyond the Jordan just before going into this wilderness **(JOHN 1:28)**, it seems likely that Jesus faced this challenge on the dry ridges west of Jericho."[17]

Those who walk up the mountain will pass the Monastery of the Temptation, a Greek Orthodox church built to commemorate the temptation. **(SEE PAGES 72–73.)**

The other way to reach the top of the mountain is to take a cable car.

Although we cannot know for certain exactly where Jesus was in the wilderness, a visit to the Judean Wilderness gives us a picture of the loneliness and desolation Jesus would have faced.

The location near Jericho makes sense as a probable location because of what the text

Early church tradition pinpoints the location at Jebel Quarantal, which is located about four miles northwest of Jericho.

THINGS TO SEE

◆ *Monastery of the Temptation:* This was built by Byzantine monks in the fourth century. It was abandoned for hundreds of years but rebuilt in the eighteenth century.

◆ *The Mount of Temptation:* Jebel Quarantal itself, the mountain overlooking the Jordan Valley and the Dead Sea.

NOTES

1. My favorite site reflections are of Bethlehem, Caesarea by the Sea, Caesarea Philippi, Capernaum, En Gedi, Jericho, Megiddo, Mount of Beatitudes, Mount Carmel, Sea of Galilee, and Temple Mount.

2. *Fodor's Essential Israel* (Fodor's Travel, 2017).

3. *Jerusalem, Israel, Petra and Sinai*, DK Eyewitness Travel (New York: Penguin Random House, 2016).

4. *Fodor's Essential Israel* (Fodor's Travel, 2017), 414.

5. *Archaeology Study Bible* (Wheaton, IL: Crossway, 2017), 1747.

6. Joseph M. Holden and Norman Geisler, *The Popular Handbook of Archaeology and the Bible (Eugene, OR: Harvest House, 2013)*, 250–51.

7. Joseph M. Holden and Norman Geisler, *The Popular Handbook of Archaeology and the Bible (Eugene, OR: Harvest House, 2013)*, 252.

8. "Where Is Golgotha, Where Jesus Was Crucified?" biblicalarchaeology.org, April 7, 2017.

9. Charles H. Dyer and Gregory A. Hatteburg, *The Christian Traveler's Guide to the Holy Land* (Chicago: Moody Publishers, 2014), 137.

10. *Archaeology Study Bible* (Wheaton, IL: Crossway, 2017).

11. John A. Beck, *Discovery House Bible Atlas* (Grand Rapids, MI: Discovery House, 2015), 271.

12. Bryan Nelson, "The World's 10 Oldest Living Trees," mnn.com, October 27, 2016.

13. *Archaeology Study Bible* (Wheaton, IL: Crossway, 2017), 1421.

14. *Fodor's Essential Israel* (Fodor's Travel, 2017), 350.

15. "About Greece," greeka.com, accessed June 5, 2020.

16. *Discovery House Atlas of the Bible* (Grand Rapids, MI: Discovery House, 2015), 243.

17. *Discovery House Atlas of the Bible* (Grand Rapids, MI: Discovery House, 2015), 242.

Help us get the word out!

Our Daily Bread Publishing exists to feed the soul
with the Word of God.

If you appreciated this book, please let others know.

- Pick up another copy to give as a gift.

- Share a link to the book or mention it on social media.

- Write a review on your blog, on a book-seller's website, or at our own site (odb.org/store).

- Recommend this book for your church, book club, or small group.

Connect with us:

 @ourdailybread

 @ourdailybread

 @ourdailybread

Our Daily Bread Publishing
PO Box 3566
Grand Rapids, Michigan 49501 USA

 books@odb.org